11.56
1/08

TRACKER
HUNTiNG DOWN
SERiAL KiLLERS

TRACKER
HUNTiNG DOWN
SERiAL KiLLERS

DR. MAURiCE GODWiN
WiTH **FRED ROSEN**

THUNDER'S MOUTH PRESS • NEW YORK

TRACKER
Hunting Down Serial Killers

© 2005 by Dr. Maurice Godwin and Fred Rosen

Published by
Thunder's Mouth Press
An imprint of Avalon Publishing Group Incorporated
245 West 17th St., 11th Floor
New York, NY 10011-5300

AVALON
publishing group incorporated

Library of Congress Cataloging-in-Publication Data is available.

ISBN 1-56025-634-6

9 8 7 6 5 4 3 2 1

Book design by Maria E. Torres

Printed in Canada
Distributed by Publishers Group West

This book is dedicated to my late father
Halford Dwight Godwin
and to my mentor the late
Thomas J. Long;
and in memory of
Pfc Fred Myatt,
killed in action 4 July 1944,
two miles west of Carentan, France.
—MG

CONTENTS

ACKNOWLEDGMENTS

MANY PEOPLE MADE THIS book possible.

First and foremost, my deepest gratitude goes to my wife, Helen, who has graciously endured my long working hours during this project, and whose encouragement, help, and support, has sustained me throughout. Also, thanks to my mother, Priscilla McKinnie, and late father, Halford Godwin, who taught me to be different.

I would also like to express my sincere gratitude to my coauthor Fred Rosen without whom I wouldn't have been involved in this book, and to Lori Perkins at Perkins Literary Management who helped make it all possible. I also wish to recognize my publisher at Thunder's Mouth Press, John Oakes, and editor Andrew Merz.

Finally, I am likewise indebted to many others, including those in the law enforcement community who so kindly gave of their time and talent.

Dr. Maurice Godwin's Web site:
www.drmauricegodwin.com

AUTHOR'S NOTE

SOME OF THE MURDER cases you are about to read are active.
That is, "the bad guys" are still out there, some still killing, some
lying low until whatever primal urge moves them again to satiation. In some of these cases, police have been honing in on prime
suspects.

In order not to compromise active cases, some names have been
changed to protect the privacy of the individuals involved. In the
cases already adjudicated, the authors have used their best judgment
to change names whenever privacy or other issues were involved,
especially for those on the periphery of a case.

FOREWORD

IF A LOVED ONE of mine were abducted, the first call I would make would be to the police. The second would be to Dr. Maurice Godwin.

When I first began corresponding with Maurice he was in the final year of his dissertation at the University of Liverpool. At first, I thought his fascination with serial killers was bizarre and morbid. I eventually realized that he was serious: pursuing serial killers is his raison d'être.

For the past decade, I have watched Maurice get involved with many of the country's highest profile serial murder cases. Unlike many of the on-air profilers, Maurice is a university professor. Anything he says or does in the public sector about serial killers has to be backed up with facts, not generalities. That's why his pioneering work in psycho-geographic profiling is the largest leap forward for law enforcement technology in the last two decades.

It has been field-tested and proven scientifically that his psycho-geographic profiles work. He can predict, within a one to two mile radius, where an active serial killer lives, and he has. During the course of writing this book, he was asked to perform a first: a reverse geographical profile, namely, where a body could be located, rather than where the killer could be found. Once again, he succeeded, when the body of University of North Dakota student Dru Sjodin was located on April 17, 2004, after a fruitless six-month search. This time, though, the searchers were armed with Godwin's reverse profile and flooded his target area; the body was found near that area.

Police departments that have been smart enough to utilize his profiles have caught these bad guys before they could kill again. But even as some choose to enter the twenty-first century, most others remain mired in the kind of antiquated, specious, cookie-cutter profiles that the FBI specializes in. In contrast, their counterparts in Scotland Yard have used psycho-geographic profiles successfully since the 1980s.

This book has been written with the hope that American law enforcement will come to finally accept that which our British cousins have, to actively utilize psycho-geographic profiling, and save lives.

Fred Rosen

PROLOGUE

Profiling On Death Row

AT FIRST GLANCE, WAVERLY, Virginia seems no different than any small town in southeastern Virginia.

Local auto dealers, fast food places, garages, markets, and other stores crowd the town's Main Street. But outside town, things change. Turn left onto Route 625 and drive exactly one mile, turn right, then go another half mile up the road. The big, ominous-looking building on the right surrounded by razor wire is Sussex State Prison. It houses Virginia's Death Row.

At the end of Death Row, in a long line of twenty-six cells that house the Commonwealth of Virginia's most vile murderers, is the room where John Allen Muhammad will spend his last moments on earth. With his ward, Lee Malvo, Muhammad formed the deadly killing team the media christened "the Sniper." At that time, most profilers thought the Sniper was one person, except me.

All the killings were the same. From out of the early morning dawn would come a shot and someone would lie dead on the pavement at a gas station or in a mall parking lot or outside a school or on the steps of a bus. During twenty-three days in October 2002, the Sniper shot thirteen people in the Washington, D.C. metro area, murdering ten. Because I'm the only psycho-geographical profiler in the United States, I found myself caught up in a whirlwind of national and international media attention. I was interviewed no less than forty times during those twenty-three days.

Since beginning my career in forensic behavioral profiling, I have received many such calls from the media. Early on, I viewed such opportunities as a chance to teach. However, I found during the Sniper shootings that many of the major TV media outlets became disappointed when what I had to say was too academic, and did not provide them with the sensationalism needed to enhance the voyeuristic appeal of the case.

In the case of the Sniper, the major TV news shows were inundated with the opinions of profilers, criminologists, clinical psychologists, and self-described sleuths. Universally, they assured listeners that when the Sniper was caught he would turn out to be a lone white male, a high school dropout with international terrorist connections.

Instead of generating more of this specious "profiling" speculation, I focused on the way in which the Snipers were traveling to carry out their shootings. These movements told me something about their travel patterns when they were not shooting and, consequently, their motive for the shootings.

As is detailed later in the book, using my psycho-geographical profiling system called Predator™, I predicted on October 8 on CNN that the Snipers would next strike in the Fredericksburg, Virginia area. I came to that conclusion through cold, hard science. Predator drew a wedge-shaped map that suggested the most likely home base and/or work area of the Snipers had a directional bias towards Northern Virginia. At the lower portion of the wedge was Fredericksburg. I was sure the Snipers would strike there. But Police Chief Charles Moose, the Montgomery County, Maryland cop in charge of the Sniper investigation, didn't listen, opting instead for another geographical profiler's opinion. No attempt was made to stake out the area with cops to prevent another homicide. And so, on October 11, the Snipers killed Kenneth Bridges, while he was pumping gas at an Exxon station in Massaponax, Virginia, just down the road from Fredericksburg.

If Chief Moose had listened, would Kenneth Bridges still be alive?

TRACKER
HUNTiNG DOWN
SERiAL KiLLERS

Chapter 1

PREDATOR™

WHEN I WAS A teenager, I bought a copy of *Helter Skelter*, Vincent Bugliosi's book about the Charles Manson murders. After reading it, I got hooked on studying criminal behavior. I knew that somehow, sometime in the future, I too would come face-to-face with the kind of evil Bugliosi had encountered.

After high school, I drifted into the 1980s, got married, divorced, and did sound and lighting for several North Carolina rock and country bands. In 1984, I decided that I wanted a career. I remembered the detectives in *Helter Skelter* and decided to go into law enforcement. I enrolled in the criminal justice program at Vance-Granville Community College. That's where I met Mr. Thomas Long.

A tall, distinctive-looking man, Mr. Long held a bachelor's degree in psychology. He was also a cop, through and through. An undercover drug agent for years, he was the rare teacher who could bring his real-world experiences into the classroom and make those experiences not only exciting but instructive.

Mr. Long took a personal interest in me and became my mentor. He helped me get accepted to the North Carolina Police

Academy, in Henderson, under the sponsorship of the Oxford Police Department. About two weeks before I was to graduate from the police academy, the chief of the Oxford PD offered me a deal: work six months doing undercover drug investigations. Once the undercover work was completed, I would be hired as a full-time police officer. I agreed.

The .25 caliber pistol was strapped to my ankle. It was hidden under my pant leg; no one could know I was packing it without giving me a good frisk. I was on the street tracking drug dealers and I figured I needed a gun that was deadly at close range. At 2:45 A.M. one Sunday in the parking lot of Oxford's Holiday Inn, I found myself wishing that I had that gun in my hand because as a drug dealer put his .44 Magnum to my head.

Undercover operations to bust a coke dealer can go smoothly if your backup is where it's supposed to be. I made the mistake of getting in a car to make a drug deal with a dealer while my partner went to the bathroom, and that was when the dealer pulled the piece and put it to my head.

"I know you're the fucking goddamn man," he said. He was so close; I could smell his foul breath.

"Shit, I ain't the damn man, I don't hang with the law," I said. "Hell, you don't want to deal with me, I'll just go somewhere else."

I guess greed got the better of suspicion.

The dealer put the pistol away and proceeded to pull out an ounce of coke from his greatcoat. We exchanged and I went on my way with the drugs. The dealer was arrested several weeks later. That's the closest I've ever come to being shot. I was scared. I would have worried had I not been.

The danger in working drug undercover in a small town or

county is that your identity can be easily discovered. You take this kind of work home with you. Every night, I would sit for thirty minutes watching my house before pulling in the driveway. The bright spot for me was that after six months of such wretched work, I was hired full-time at the Oxford PD and worked as a dispatcher, patrol officer, and Breathalyzer operator until 1987, when I left to go back to school.

My future as a criminal profiler was sealed one wintry night in 1993. By that time, I had received my associate's and bachelor's degrees and had decided to enter academia. I was studying for my master's of science in criminology at Indiana State University, in Terre Haute, when I saw a Discovery Channel show entitled *Murder in Mind.* The featured segment dealt with a new profiling degree program at the University of Liverpool in England. It was called investigative psychology, and the professor who had developed the course of study was Dr. David Canter. I applied there and was accepted into the program.

The purpose of my investigative psychology research at Liverpool University was to find a better way to classify the crime scene behavior of serial murderers. The investigative psychology approach taught me that actions speak louder than words, that what criminals do reveals more than what any of them can tell us in an interview.

In 1995, I visited various police departments in the United States to collect serial murder data for my doctoral dissertation. One source of my data was the Attorney General's Office for the State of Washington. With the assistance of Dr. Robert Keppel, I was able to obtain data on serial killers through the state's Homicide Investigating Tracking System (HITS).

My research was based on the collection and critical analysis of over 100,000 data points gathered from more than 500 solved serial murder case files. I then relied on a mathematical algorithm that is able to make sense of seemingly random pieces of crime scene information by placing them in context and allowing interrelationships among them to emerge.

Each case had about two hundred different variables that could potentially be used to profile a killer. These included mundane information, such as the sex, race, and age of both the offender and the victim; the location of the crime; previous crimes committed; and the education and employment history of the criminal. The data also included information specific to the crime, such as the cause of death. Was the individual murdered by strangulation, decapitation, drowning, or poison? If the victim was raped, did the act occur before or after death, and was it anal or vaginal rape? These variables made up only a small fraction of the types of data looked at.

When all the data points from the five hundred-plus cases were analyzed, the result was an intricate, scientific profiling system—a set of clear guidelines for identifying critical information at a crime scene, determining salient behaviors of serial killers, and scientifically classifying offenders for profiling purposes. An important part of this system is analyzing criminal mobility and the relationship between offenders' home bases and their target areas.

The use of locations in predicting specific anchor points can be traced back to 1854 and Dr. John Snow's pioneering geographical data analysis. Using this method for the first time in history, Snow induced the origin of the spread of cholera in the drinking water in London. He was able to prove using through geographic data points how cholera spread through contaminated water.

While investigating the epidemic, Snow began plotting the location of deaths related to cholera on a map showing which of · two water companies supplied water to the infected homes. A higher concentration of cholera was found in the region of town supplied by the company that drew its water from the downstream of the two locations. It's possible this source, or some nearby part of the system, had been contaminated by the city's sewage.

Snow found that in one particular location, near the intersection of Cambridge and Broad Street, up to five hundred deaths from cholera had occurred within a single ten-day period. Panic-stricken officials followed Snow's advice to remove the handle of the Broad Street pump that supplied the water to this neighborhood. Thus the epidemic was contained. Snow's pioneering work saved lives.

Snow's analysis could be considered by today's technology a type of spatial analysis using a paper geographic information system (GIS). A GIS is an organized collection of spatial and geographic data, designed to capture, store, update, manipulate, analyze, and display all forms of geographically referenced information. Some have claimed Snow's Broad Street map is the first known example of a GIS, even though it was performed with a pen and paper. Whether or not Snow's system can be called a GIS, his cholera work in the 1850s is often pointed to as the start of modern epidemiology and geographic profiling.

The next big development in using geography to track killers was the use of a simple computerized method of spatial analysis to predict the location of a suspect's home, based on where crimes had occurred. This can be traced to the late British forensic biologist Dr. Stuart Kind. In 1981, Kind developed what could be considered the first-ever geographical profile, during the course of the Yorkshire Ripper serial murders in Leeds, England.

Sometime around 3 A.M. on December 9, 1980, after less than two weeks on the Yorkshire Ripper serial murder case, Kind telephoned down to the reception desk at the hotel in Leeds where he and four senior detectives had set up a makeshift command post and asked for some graph paper and a pencil. Over the next few hours, Kind made a series of calculations using techniques he had learned as a wartime navigator in the British Royal Air Force.

The Yorkshire Ripper had murdered thirteen women over a five-year period. Kind plotted the dates and times of the attacks on a map, with the aim of determining their "center of gravity." He realized the killer needed darkness to cover his crimes and was trying to mislead the police as to his home base. But Kind also knew it was possible that the Ripper needed not only to leave the scene of his crimes as soon as possible after they were committed but also to return home the same night to avoid suspicion and capture. He therefore deduced that the earlier in the evening an attack happened, the farther away from home the killer was.

From a series of calculations run through the computer at the Home Office Central Research Establishment at Aldermaston, where Stuart Kind was the director, he was able to tell his colleagues that the Yorkshire Ripper lived somewhere between Shipley and Bingley in West Yorkshire. The focus of the investigation then shifted to suspects in the Bradford area. One of the suspects was a truck driver named Peter Sutcliffe who lived midway between the towns suggested by Kind.

Two weeks later Sutcliffe was arrested in Sheffield by two beat officers. In 1981, he was found guilty of murder by a majority verdict of ten to two and was sentenced to life imprisonment with a mandatory term of thirty years. He was later determined to be insane and is currently housed at Broadmoor Hospital in England.

The technique that Kind used to predict the residence of the Yorkshire Ripper later became known as geographical profiling. The first use of geographical profiling in the United States was in 1985, when the late Dr. Milton B. Newton Jr., a geographer at Louisiana

State University in Baton Rouge, published his study of serial killers based upon a geographic analysis of their crimes.

While I was at Liverpool University, I read about Newton's geo-forensic analysis of serial killers. I found the idea of using crime locations to predict where a suspect lives exciting and, more importantly, an applicable investigative tool for catching serial killers. From that day forward, I was hooked. I was going to spend my life as a modern-day tracker.

One of the most interesting applications proposed by Newton is the use of geo-forensic analysis for the defense of individuals who might be wrongly accused of serial murders. Dr. Newton suggested that it is unlikely that a man falsely accused of a being a serial killer will live in the "buffer zone," which is defined as a geographical area around an offender's home where no crimes have been committed. He surmised that if at the time of the serial murders the accused did not live in the same neighborhood(s) as those of the crime scenes, then the prosecution should have the burden of showing how and why the accused went to the "center of gravity" of the murders to begin and end each journey to crime.

The logic behind this defense strategy, in the absence of other damning prosecution evidence like DNA or fingerprint identification, is that if the defendant has no home in or near the center of gravity of the crimes and is not known to have committed other murders in the series, then the prosecution should have the burden of showing how the other crime data can be accounted for.

Between 1982 and 1987 in North London, rapist/murderer John Duffy attacked his victims at night, on or near railway stations. Duffy's preferred victims were fifteen-to nineteen-year-old girls whom he surprised while they waited for the train. After the sexual assaults, he would use a garrote to finish off his victims, tying a "Spanish windlass," a knot typically used by carpenters to hold wood together.

Duffy made some attempts to clean up the crime scenes, but police almost always found semen traces and, in some cases, small footprints (Duffy was a small man, only five foot four). One of Duffy's rape victims survived but due to her traumatized condition after the incident was not able to give investigators a good description of her attacker. She would later tell police about his eyes, calling him the "Man with the Laser Eyes." Police were so frustrated after three violent attacks occurred in one night in 1985 that they organized "Operation Hart," which was to become the largest manhunt in Britain since the Yorkshire Ripper case. Police had identified John Duffy as a suspect in the series, and had questioned him at one point regarding the deaths, but they had no proof. He was in the Operation Hart computer, but he was near the bottom of the list, which contained the names of thousands of potential suspects.

In need of an alternative approach to help solve the case, Scotland Yard solicited the help of Dr. David Canter, the professor who had developed the investigative psychology program at Liverpool University, where I had done research after leaving Indiana State in 1993. This was a refreshing change. Rarely if ever do U.S. law enforcement agencies turn to a college professor for expert advice, and usually only if the case is very cold. I found, however, during the five years that I lived in England, that the big brass in the British Police were often receptive to academic researchers—many even attended annual investigative psychology conferences to learn about new investigative techniques.

Professor Canter developed a psychological and geographical profile of the North London killer based on witness statements, crime scene reports, and information about where the attacks had taken place. Canter's geographical profile accurately predicted that the killer lived in the Kilburn/Cricklewood area of northwest London. The profile said that the killer was married, childless, and had an unhappy married life. When Canter's psychological profile was run alongside the Operation Hart database, which contained details of the unsolved crimes and possible suspects, it came up with a computer match for John Duffy.

He was immediately arrested at his mother's house, where police also obtained enough forensic evidence to prosecute him. Duffy was eventually convicted of two murders, four rapes, and sentenced to thirty years. Canter's profile combined for the first time principles of environmental psychology with spatial research in constructing a geographical profile. This approach helped shape my future research in geographical profiling.

I see the journey to crime as an expression of a complex interaction between the offender, his or her background characteristics, knowledge, and perceptions, and the location and type of target. Serial killers work on the basis of perceived risks, rewards, opportunities, and attractions. I learned early on that the actual nature of the location selected for the murder may be indicative of the purpose and experiences of the offender, that there may be patterns of space typical of different criminals, relating to where they are living at the time of their crimes.

I came to understand that local modifications (for example, the landscape of areas such as central business areas, bridges, rivers, etc.) could indeed distort the travel patterns of criminals. I began to test this hypothesis by collecting spatial data on serial killers and carrying out research. Using LSU geographer Milton Newton's idea that the locations where victims go missing from tell us more about the location of the suspect's home than any other crime location, I coined the term *psycho-geographic profiling.*

Psycho-geographic profiling is based on the collection and critical analysis of over 100,000 data points and 200 different crime scene actions that could be used to profile the perpetrator. Instead of relying on interviews with murderers, I studied specific pieces of behavioral information available from the crime scene or case file. This is what differentiates what I do from the type of profiling done by the FBI. Using the geographical profiling software program I developed, called Predator, I can accurately predict where a serial killer is going to strike before he does, as well as his "home area."

A typical prediction area is wedge-shaped, similar to a slice of pie. Analyses have shown that there is an 80 percent probability that the criminal lives or works within that wedge, and a 50 percent probability that he lives or works in the narrow tip of the wedge. The Predator program, however, does not hone in on a single street or house, but in a narrow area in which the serial criminal lives. This is the area in which police should search for the perpetrator.

The search area could include the perpetrator's home, or some other anchor point that may have a strong significance for the perpetrator such as his girlfriend's home, parents' home, or work location. Predator allows the criminal's spatial movements to be modeled from all directions, no matter if they are moving in or out of the area. This process also allows Predator to profile serial killers who travel considerable distances, in addition to killers whose crimes remain local.

Each killer's crime locations and their respective latitude and longitude coordinates are entered into Predator. Once this task is completed, all these coordinates are converted into The Universal Transverse Mercator (UTM) grid system. UTM coordinates serve to express the unique, absolute location of each crime event, and are impartial and independently verifiable. Converting the latitude and longitude coordinates into the UTM coordinate system allows the data to be entered into the Predator geographical profiling program.

The next step is to calculate the angle degrees and distance, between crime locations, which involves first determining the size of the actual crime area under study. For each crime series, the distance between the furthest northing and easting crime locations is measured and recorded. Each distance is then entered separately into the Predator program, which then creates, on the computer screen, a scale of the actual crime area in miles or kilometers. For each event, the northing and easting UTM coordinate serves to express the unique, absolute location of each crime event. Equally important, the UTM coordinate system is impartial, and the values of locations are independently verifiable.

After entering into a spreadsheet built into the Predator system the UTM coordinates for each location for each crime series, the geographical program plots each of the crime locations on the computer screen. I analyze each case separately. Predator incorporates a separate function for calculating the angle degrees between crimes.

When you put all this together, what you have is a robust, induction-driven profiling system. Now all I needed was the right opportunity to show that it worked.

CHAPTER **2**

THE RALEiGH
SERiAL KiLLER

BENEATH THE POSH SPOTS of Raleigh, North Carolina, hidden under the city's steel bridges, homeless men and women eat, sleep, sing, and reminisce about better days. They say life is hard.

"People get drunk, and then they get crazy," said twenty-six-year-old Antonio Zuniga, a migrant worker who once lived in a tent near the Amtrak station.

Nearby, renovated warehouses have been turned into trendy nightspots and restaurants. But when darkness falls by the tracks, some men and women prostitute themselves, some shoot up, and some become victims and die.

Some, however, get lucky and survive, like Patricia Crump. Patricia Crump had been using cocaine off and on for about thirteen years. Occasionally she would exchange sex for crack or money. On October 25, 1995, Crump left her boyfriend's house in Raleigh to buy a pack of cigarettes. According to court transcripts, Crump remembered being at a concrete tunnel that goes under Martin Luther King Boulevard which connects Chavis Park on one side to an area of Old Garner Road on the other side. She recalled walking past the tunnel with two men. The two men were talking about sex, and one of them suggested that they go into the tunnel. When she refused to go, she was pushed into the tunnel. One man grabbed her by the throat and started choking her while she was backed up against the wall of the tunnel. She could not move or escape. He got on top of her and started pushing down her pants while still keeping one hand on her throat. At this point, Crump blacked out.

The next morning, October 26, Raleigh police officer David German was dispatched to the scene, arriving at 9:13. Crump had no clothing on the bottom half of her body except for a white sock on her left foot. There was blood all over the wall and on the floor of the tunnel. She had a fractured nose and facial bone fractures. Her eyes were swollen shut. She had a couple of gashes on the side of her head and cuts and bruises on her arms and legs.

The evidence at the scene appeared to indicate that she had been beaten with a beer bottle and sexually assaulted. The police would search vainly for her assailant.

Audrey Hall had used crack cocaine off and on since 1985 and, in May 1996, was actively involved in the Raleigh drug scene. On various occasions, she too exchanged sex for money. Hall had a friend, Frank Weller, who lived in southeast Raleigh. Occasionally, when she visited Weller at his home, she would use crack.

On Saturday May 25, Hall went to Weller's house at about 5:00 P.M. She had been smoking crack all day and continued to there, where she stayed overnight. In the morning, an acquaintance of Weller's, John Williams Jr., arrived at his house. Williams, who knew Hall, wanted to see her. Weller woke Hall up to tell her Williams was looking for her. Williams came in and sat down beside Hall on the couch. He asked Hall if she wanted to smoke some cocaine, to which she responded yes. Williams asked Hall if she knew where he could score some. Hall replied yes, and they left Weller's house about 3:00 P.M. to get stoned.

Hall intended to take Williams to a crack house that was about two blocks from Weller's house. Williams said he still had some cocaine and asked if there was some place where they could smoke it. Hall took Williams to a wooded area that was adjacent to South Wilmington Street, near some railroad tracks. When they got to the woods, Hall took a "hit" of Williams's cocaine. Williams motioned for her to walk in front of him.

When she did, Williams grabbed her by the throat, squeezed tightly, and threw her on the ground. Williams began choking Hall and told her to take her clothes off. Williams threatened her with a box cutter if she didn't do what he asked. He made her walk farther into the woods, get on her knees and perform oral sex on him.

Hall later told police that Williams said, "If you don't do what I tell you to do, you will wind up dead."

Williams pushed Hall on her back, stuffed his penis down her throat, and ejaculated. While holding the box cutter, Williams continued to choke and assault her. Then he tied her up and left. After Hall began screaming for help, someone heard her and called police. Raleigh police officer Kevin Carswell and two other officers were dispatched to the wooded area. The officers eventually found Hall tied with her hands stretched over her head, nude except for a dirty white sock on her right foot. Officer Carswell later testified that it was apparent that the victim was dragged to the place where she was found.

Hall was able to identify her attacker as John Williams, a black man wearing black jeans and a black shirt and carrying a backpack. "You'll likely find John Williams at Frank Weller's house at 203 Bragg Street," she added.

Taken to Wake County Medical Center, Hall was treated for

facial trauma and cuts and abrasions on her hands face and back. Vaginal swabs were taken. Subsequent blood samples from Williams were later subjected to DNA analysis. The analysis by the North Carolina State Bureau of Investigation (SBI) crime lab revealed a DNA banding pattern that was consistent with a mixture of the DNA profile for Audrey Hall and John Williams. Additional DNA testing by another lab revealed that sperm from the vaginal swabbing had genetic characteristics that were consistent with characteristics possessed by Williams. Ultimately, this testing excluded 99.99 percent of the world's population.

Like Patricia Crump, Audrey Hall was just happy to be alive.

Vicki Whitaker had used crack but she was not an addict. According to her testimony, she met John Williams at a store on Davie Street around 8:00 one night in July 1996.

Whitaker was walking toward a bar on Hillsborough Street, near the North Carolina State University campus, when Williams came up behind her and started walking with her. She later testified that she told Williams she needed to use a bathroom. He walked her to a location near a warehouse where a truck trailer was situated. She said that she would not use the bathroom there, and that was when Williams grabbed her by the throat.

The two started to fight and ended up on the ground. Williams told her to take her pants off, ripped her shirt and got her pants unbuttoned. He put both hands around her neck, choked her, and told her that he was going to kill her if she did not take her pants off. She managed to kick him in the groin, and he ran away.

Whitaker had many scratches on her neck as a result of the attack. She later testified that she did not report the matter to the police until six or seven months later because she was on probation at the time of the incident. She was not supposed to be drinking or out at that time of the night.

Kimberly Warren was homeless and unemployed in November 1996. She would stay at the ASK, a store on Harrington Street that offered services as a temporary employment agency, sleeping in the van that belonged to the business. William Hargrove, a friend of Warren's, was responsible for the van and drove people to work in it, including John Williams.

Hargrove had introduced Warren and Williams in the van. She was using crack cocaine daily during this time. After they were introduced, Williams indicated that he wanted oral sex in exchange for some crack. On some occasions, Kimberly had exchanged sex for drugs, but she turned down Williams this time because she already had some crack.

About three weeks later, Warren saw Williams on Harrington Street near the Greyhound bus station. He asked her if she wanted to get high or if she wanted some money. She responded that she wanted to get high. He told her to wait down the street near the 42nd Street Oyster Bar. Williams met her there a few minutes later, and they walked to a warehouse near Hargett Street. They climbed a fence and went toward a parked trailer.

Williams opened the sliding door on the back of the trailer and they climbed inside, and closing the door halfway behind them. As he began to unwrap the plastic off the crack, he said to Warren, "Bitch, take your clothes off." When Warren refused, Williams put his hands around her neck, lifted her up, and slammed her against the wall of the trailer. He kept one hand around her neck and brandished a sharp object in his other hand.

She struggled, managed to get his hand away from her throat, and screamed. Once she screamed, Williams ran away. Warren walked back to Harrington Street and told Hargrove what had happened, which he later corroborated at trial, but she did not report the assault to the police. Her neck was scratched as a result of the incident.

Three or four months later, Hargrove pointed Kimberly Warren out to a Raleigh police officer and told the officer that she had told him that John Williams had attacked her. She later identified Williams in a lineup as her attacker.

By that time, it was much too late.

Patricia Anne Ashe lived in Raleigh's Walnut Terrace with her parents but had drifted around downtown neighborhoods for many years. During drug arrests in 1994 and 1995, she told police she was a transient, finding infrequent work as a cashier in local restaurants.

Ashe, thirty-three, was a habitual crack cocaine user. On January 7, 1996, Officer G. M. Wright of the Raleigh Police Department was dispatched to the 1500 block of South Blount Street, where he found a black male, Rodney Bass, waving to get his attention. Bass stated that he had seen a naked woman around the back of the building. It had been snowing and sleeting off and on throughout the day.

Wright found Ashe's body on a bench, badly beaten and covered with snow. Underneath her, Wright observed, was pristine ground. The cop saw a set of footprints near the body. These footprints did not get close enough to indicate that the person who left them could have touched her. The location was not far from the railroad tracks.

The victim's body was on the lower portion of the bench, with her feet and lower body hanging off the edge. Her legs were completely off the end of the bench, slightly spread, and her knees were bent. She had no clothes on except white socks. A thermal long-sleeve T-shirt was folded up under her buttocks, a pair of jeans folded under her head. A couple of crack pipes and a lighter lay underneath or just to the side of the bench.

Dr. John Butts, North Carolina chief medical examiner, performed an autopsy on Ashe's body. Based upon the scrapes and scratches on both sides of her neck, as well as some on the front part of her neck, and the broken hyoid bone in her throat, the ME concluded death was due to strangulation. Multiple scratches and scrapes on her neck indicated that she had struggled with her attacker.

Dawn Marie Grandy, thirty, gave birth to seven children, the first when she was nineteen, but her drug habit made her incapable of being the mother she wanted to be. Due to her drug problems, which had grown worse during the eleven years since her mother had moved to Raleigh from Connecticut, Grandy's children had ended up in the care of social services.

Grandy's problems also included violent boyfriends. She was granted a domestic violence protective order in 1994 because, she said when she applied for the order, the man she was living with had slapped her, threatened to kill her, and threatened to burn the house down. The boyfriend had been out of prison for less than a year for beating a man to death under a bridge in South Raleigh in 1990.

Despite her crack cocaine addiction, Grandy took housekeeping jobs when she could get them through an employment agency. She was no doubt aware that a killer was loose on the streets of Raleigh, and that her neighbor Patricia Anne Ashe had been found dead in January 1996. A transient found Grandy's body one

Sunday afternoon at a homeless camp near railroad tracks under the Morgan Street Bridge, nude except for a pair of high-top trainer shoes and white socks.

Grandy had been raped, and a condom was found in her vagina. The ME said the cause of death was acute aortic rupture of the main vessel to the heart, brought on by blunt chest trauma. Near the body, police investigators found a possible murder weapon, a brick. Footprints were found on her head and side. Grandy, too, had been strangled. The absence of ligature marks probably meant the killer had used his hands.

Patricia Gwendolyn Woods lived in a matchbox of a wood-shingled house. From her front porch, she had a great view of the tombstone skyline spread out across the street at the Oakwood Cemetery. It was something she saw each day as she eased down the plank steps to Oakwood Avenue, where the dirt pathway called Selwyn Alley disappears behind a row of tiny houses.

The thirty-eight-year-old Woods had lived off and on in the Raleigh area for several years. A married assembly line worker at a furniture manufacturing plant, she had moved back to Raleigh full-time from her hometown of Louisburg less than two months before.

Woods had a drug problem. She had pleaded guilty in April 1996 to a felony charge of crack cocaine possession, and on June 7 admitted to obtaining unemployment benefits illegally. The housing authority in Raleigh had evicted her from her fifty-seven-dollar-a-month two-bedroom apartment. She had only recently moved into the house by the cemetery on Oakwood Avenue.

On June 13, 1996, Woods's body was found by groundskeepers in Oakwood Cemetery. She was wearing a bra, which was unhooked, and an ankle bracelet. According to the ME's report, several upper teeth were missing. There were multiple abrasions and contusions to the face, head and neck areas. Smaller abrasions and contusions were found on the victim's hands, forearms, lower legs and back. There were no skull fractures. There was no evidence of external genitalia injury, although she had been anally assaulted.

The ME ruled the cause of death was manual or possible ligature strangulation with an article of clothing from the victim. Other contributing factors to her death were multiple blunt traumas to the face and head.

The body was found at a construction site on the Martin Luther King Boulevard extension project near Dawson Street in Raleigh. Whoever she was, she was naked and had no ID. She was also missing one hand. Decomposition was far enough along that her bones were easily seen through her rotting flesh. Her clothing had apparently been scattered nearby.

After an autopsy, the ME said that she had been strangled, which was the probable cause of death. Investigators called in Brit Ponsit, a forensic anthropologist from the University of North Carolina at Charlotte. Ponsit was called in to obtain partial fingerprints, which eventually led to the identification of the body as Cynthia Brown, thirty-two. Brown had an extensive record of drug, theft, and prostitution arrests.

On December 23, 1996, Deborah Elliott spoke with her sister Eileen about her Christmas plans. She was supposed to go to their other sister Judy's house at about 1:00 P.M. on Christmas Eve and stay until the next day. Deborah Elliott never arrived, and was reported missing.

Police found that Elliott was a crack user and prostitute. When prostitutes and/or drug addicts are murdered, a problem police have is that because of the victims' peripatetic lifestyle, it's hard to reconstruct the timeline prior to the murder. But police did find someone who had seen Elliott. His name was Tommie Agee, the owner/manager of the Swoboda Street Mini Mart in Raleigh, near Shamsky Square. Elliott had been to Swoboda's on the morning of December 24.

Two days later, on December 26, construction worker Bobby Pfeill was working at a building on North West Street near downtown Raleigh that was formerly part of Pine State Creamery. Pfeill had the responsibility of making sure the doors were locked in the creamery's three bays. While making his rounds, Pfeill discovered Deborah Elliott in the second bay, lying facedown. Except for her shoes and socks, she was naked. Other than one left shoeprint, few forensic clues were found at the Elliott crime scene.

While the rest of the state recovered from the Christmas holiday, on December 27, Dr. D. E. Scarborough autopsied Deborah Elliott. The medical examiner found that Elliott had a large laceration over the right side of her forehead; her underlying skull was fractured. She had hemorrhaged over the surface of her brain, and there was actual tearing of the brain relating to the laceration and fracture in her forehead. There were numerous abrasions and scrapes over her arms and legs and substantial bruising, hemorrhaging, and swelling around both of her eyes. She also had multiple scratches over the front and right side of her neck and a small amount of hemorrhaging on the left side of the larynx in the neck.

The ME ruled the cause of death to be blunt trauma to the head.

* * *

While in Liverpool, I had been reading about the Raleigh Serial Murders for over a year. Prior to this string of unsolved murders, Raleigh homicide detectives had had an impressive homicide clearance rate. That is, they had a successful record of solving murders. However, they had never investigated a serial murder case, defined as the killing of three or more individuals on different dates, with a cooling off period between murders.

During the course of the Raleigh Serial Killer investigation, police had conducted 6,000 interviews, beefed up downtown patrols, and tried to assure the public that the five women had not been murdered by a single individual. One Raleigh detective said that the police had at least three separate suspects for three of the murders. Raleigh chief of police Mitchell W. Brown went so far as to say that no special task force was needed to focus on the murders.

While acknowledging that the circumstances and causes of the deaths were similar, North Carolina chief medical examiner John Butts stated publicly that the crimes lacked a signature behavior common to each murder that would point to a serial murderer. But the public wasn't buying it. People on the street began speaking openly about a serial killer in their midst. Investigators tried to calm the public's speculation, but despite police claims, there were similarities in the Raleigh murders.

All of the victims—those who were slain and sexually assaulted—were black women living lives on the margins of society, abusing drugs, frequenting the downtown street scenes. Four of the victims were found in close proximity to each other near railroad tracks running through the center of the city. The other was found in Oakwood Cemetery northeast of downtown. None of the slain women were slashed or stabbed. The autopsy reports on the first four homicides indicated that the victims had been beaten and strangled. Two or possibly three of the victims knew each other. All but one died less than a mile from their homes. With the unsolved murders of the five, it appeared obvious to everyone in the Capital City but the cops that they had a serial killer on the loose.

CHAPTER 3

"ACADEMIC SLEUTH MADE STARTLING PREDICTIONS"

BY FEBRUARY 1997, I was in the third year of my PhD work at Liverpool University. I was anxious to work an active case to see if my research would work in practice. That's when I got the e-mail from home.

Sam Archer, a crime reporter from the *News & Observer,* a statewide newspaper located in Raleigh, contacted me about developing a profile on the five unsolved murders in the city. Since I'm from the Raleigh area, and my research was on serial killers, to Archer I seemed like a natural to work the case.

Archer told me that there was a series of unsolved murders of black females in Raleigh, and that the Raleigh investigators had only recently set up a task force to look into the homicides. Archer felt that the police were convinced the murders were not linked. Could I provide a criminal profile and a geographical profile in the unsolved murders? It was the first opportunity in the real world to put into play what I now felt was my calling.

I agreed, but only if I could get copies of the police reports, autopsy reports, and any forensic analysis results that had been carried out on evidence found at the crime scenes. I also requested that the final profiling report be given to the Raleigh investigators. Not only did the police need it, but I wanted them to be forced into using it regardless of whether they believed it or not. I knew I could save lives if I was correct.

I was assured that what case information could be gathered would be mailed to me in Liverpool and the profile report would be given to detectives. Seven days later, I received most of the requested case information except for the results of any forensic analysis; that information was not available. Nonetheless, I had plenty of case information on which to build a profile.

My three profiling tasks were:

- DETERMINE WHICH MURDERS, IF ANY, WERE LINKED
- DEVELOP A PSYCHOLOGICAL PROFILE OF THE POSSIBLE KILLER
- CREATE A GEOGRAPHICAL PROFILE DESCRIBING THE LIKELY LOCATION WHERE THE KILLER RESIDES

The crime of serial murder poses many difficult problems for law enforcement officials. Most murders are committed by killers who know the victims. Because most serial murders are stranger-to-stranger homicides and lack forensic evidence or witnesses, criminal investigators are left to deal with a very large number of suspects, with only a small probability of the offender being included. Due to police inability to link or connect offenders or offenses, serial murderers are usually caught by chance or coincidence. Rarely, if ever, are serial murderers caught through investigative efforts.

This inability to link a series of crimes is often referred to as "linkage blindness." Serial murder researcher Dr. Steven Egger coined the term. Egger defines linkage blindness as the "nearly total lack of sharing or coordinating of investigative information and the lack of adequate networking by law enforcement agencies." This inability to share information applies to the failure of law enforcement agencies to share case information across city, county, and state jurisdictional lines. This is a dirty little secret of law enforcement; even in serial killer cases, cooperation among agencies is uncommon.

In the Raleigh case, the cops failed to recognize links between murders. I call this failure *ampliative blindness*. In other words, while it is important for police to share similar case information on unsolved crimes with other police agencies, it is equally important for investigators to first recognize linked offenses *in their own jurisdiction carried out by a single offender*.

Raleigh detectives sought the aid of the FBI's Violent Criminal Apprehension Program (VICAP) to see if the murders were linked. Computerized databases such as VICAP, which stores, manages, and links crimes, actually play only a minor role in helping police link crimes. In fact, in this case the results were not positive; VICAP, the FBI's own linking data base, found no connections between the murders.

I found this odd. I realized that VICAP probably wouldn't find similar murders in other regions of North Carolina or other states, but VICAP should have found links between the five unsolved murders in Raleigh. I spoke with several of the investigators who worked the Williams case.

"Didn't VICAP at least link the five unsolved murders that you were investigating?" I asked. They replied, "No, VICAP could find no link between just the Raleigh murders."

Relying on MO factors is the main reason why police investigators and systems such as VICAP fail to link crimes. The traditional use of modus operandi (MO), as a basis for linking offenses, is premised on the investigator's deductive reasoning that the MO is static and uniquely characteristic to a particular offender. Traditionally, MO is defined as distinctive actions that link crimes together.

Using MO to classify or link crimes is rather unreliable, as it does not take into account the many offense dynamics that can affect a change in an offender's behavior. Such influences include changing victim reaction from offense to offense. The offender's MO can also change over time as a result of a number of factors, including experience. When committing crimes such as rape or murder, experience leads to refinements or changes in conduct so as to facilitate the completion of the crime.

These refinements can have a number of causes, including the result of being arrested, or victim response causing the offender to change his way of dealing with his victim and therefore any future victims. The change in behavior could be attributed to factors such as maintaining control over the victim by the use of a weapon or, for example, a rapist progressing to murder in order to avoid identification.

Another way police attempt to deduce what occurred in a series of murders is to look at those actions that are unique across the offense series. The unique behavior that serial murderers repeatedly show at their crime scenes is referred to as the killer's *psychological signature*. The FBI has explained these unique crime patterns as the killer's traits. Instead, I believe that traits are inferred from behavior and cannot be turned around and used to explain behavior.

A signature behavior is not going to be present in every murder scene, due to disturbances during the course of an offense, an unanticipated victim response, or because the body of the victim has decomposed prior to its discovery. In such cases, the signature aspect has been destroyed. The point is, determining the underlying structure of a killer's behavior requires extensive scientific analysis beyond any that is currently in use by police forces.

* * *

Deciding on the links between offender patterns or crimes is one of the most crucial decisions faced by any investigator. Recognizing similar patterns early on can lead to increased resources for the police agency, improve clearance rates, and ultimately save lives. Positive linkage can also help narrow down the search area for potential suspects.

Using information from the Raleigh crime scene files and autopsy reports, the following crime actions were chosen for my link analysis using a computer program called Smallest Space Analysis (SSA):

- LIGATURE
- SEMEN FOUND AT CRIME SCENE
- BLUDGEON
- RESTRAINT OF VICTIM
- WEAPON HANDS/FEET
- ANAL PENETRATION
- VAGINAL PENETRATION
- CLOTHING SCATTERED
- NUDE VICTIM

SSA assigns a percentage to measure the association between crime scene actions. SSA maps actions that have a relationship and those that have no relationship.

For example, in a series of four homicides, if a killer performed similar actions in his first two murders, but not in his third and fourth, then the first two crimes will have higher percentages reflecting a relationship between the two offenses, while the remaining crimes will have lower percentages reflecting little or no relationship. This process is more reliable than deductive conclusions based on mere hunches, work experience, or so-called gut feelings.

My analysis used crime scene actions from fifteen serial murder cases, ten of which were solved, committed by separate killers and from different regions in the United States. The ten solved murders were randomly selected by a research associate of mine at Liverpool University and had no relationship to the Raleigh murders. The case selection process was blind. In other words, I had no prior knowledge of the crimes, how they were arranged, or which offenses were linked prior to the analysis. I was aware that five of the fifteen murders represented the Raleigh unsolved murders but did not know which order they were in.

All the murders were examined together, not as separate events. The objective of the analysis was to predict which murders were linked. The results of my scientific link analysis using SSA are shown in the table below.

	A1	A2	A3	B1	B2	B3
A1						
A2	0.04					
A3	0.13	0.04				
B1	0.09	0.12	0.26			
B2	0.03	0.20	0.15	0.23		
B3		0.20	0.04	0.32	0.26	
C1	0.04	0.30*	0.08	0.35	0.24	0.50
C2		0.08	0.07	0.12	0.28	0.25
C3	0.03	0.28	0.10	0.22	0.45*	0.25
C4	0.07	0.20	0.11	0.12	0.08*	0.14
D1		0.20	0.04	0.25	0.26	0.47*
D2		0.23	0.10	0.22	0.35*	0.30*
D3		0.23	0.10	0.22	0.35*	0.30*
D4		0.23	0.10	0.22	0.35*	0.30*
D5		0.23	0.10	0.22	0.35*	0.30*

Number of Killers – 6 – Number of murders = 15   Number of crime scene actions – 9

Each number in the squares is a percentage reflecting a relationship between crime scene actions. The shaded squares are percentages, which show a relationship between murders carried out by the same killer. The squares that are not shaded reflect murders that have no significant relationship, and the empty squares indicate no relationship. The majority of offenses show no co-occurrence, which would be expected because the behaviors in the offenses differ and the crimes were committed by different serial killers. In a few instances, a relationship was found between offenses that were not related. These findings were minor and did not create any difficulty in my linking predications.

C1	C2	C3	C4	D1	D2	D3	D4
0.29							
0.19	0.06						
0.60	0.32	0.04					
0.12	0.12	0.11	0.07				
0.39*	0.50*	0.12	0.20	0.43*			
0.39*	0.50*	0.12	0.20	0.43	1.00*		
0.39*	0.50*	0.12	0.20	0.43	1.00	1.00	
0.39*	0.50*	0.12	0.20	0.43	1.00*	1.00	1.00

A minimum percentage of 0.30 is required to show a strong relationship between crimes. The number 0.30 means that 30 percent of the crime scene actions in any two murders are similar. Percentages of 0.30 or higher are highlighted by an asterisk and shaded. The analysis did not tell me which specific actions were linked, though. In order to determine this, I had to look back at the original crimes for comparisons. The analysis did, however, tell me which murders were linked.

I accurately predicted that murders A1, A2, and A3, were committed by three separate serial murderers. I based my conclusions on the rather low percentages, 0.04, 0.13, and 0.04, indicating that these murders had little relationship to each other. I concluded that the next series of murders, B1, B2, and B3, were committed by the same serial murderer. I based my conclusions on the high percentages in the shaded areas between B1, B2, and B3, which indicated that the murders have a relationship.

The percentage between B1 and B3 is 0.32, indicating a strong relationship between the crimes. In the two remaining links, B1 to B2 and B2 to B3, while the percentages 0.23 and 0.26 are less than the required 0.30, the percentages are very close to the minimum, indicating that some type of a relationship exists. Consequently, considering the overall percentage levels, I accurately concluded that the same killer committed B1, B2, and B3.

In the next analysis, I concluded four murders were linked: C1, C2, C3, and C4. The shaded squares that represent these four murders are located in the middle of the matrix. The percentage .29, between murder C1 and C2, although lower than .30, still suggests a probable link. The .60 and .32 relationships between C1 and C4, and between C2 and C4, are more emphatic indicators. The remaining low percentages, .04, .06, .19, suggested that the actions in these three murders differed considerably, although they were committed by the same killer.

The final five murders, D1 to D5, represented the five unsolved female murders in Raleigh. The analysis showed that they were indeed strongly linked to each other, as I had predicted. The percentages are shown in the very last squares located at the bottom right of the matrix. The 1.00 percentages indicate a perfect relationship between these murders.

My analysis concluded that the murders of Deborah Jean Elliott (D4) and Patricia Ann Ashe (D5) were linked, which was later confirmed by DNA analysis. I also determined that the remaining three murders, of Dawn Marie Grandy (D1), Cynthia Brown (D2), and Patricia Gwendolyn Woods (D3), were linked not only to each other but also to those of Deborah Elliott and Patricia Ann Ashe. With my analysis complete, I knew that the same killer was responsible for all five deaths. My link analysis aided me in developing a psychological profile of the likely individual who murdered these five women.

The following profile was developed on April 15, 1997, and e-mailed to the *News & Observer* before John Williams Jr. was arrested. Copies of all profiles were provided to Raleigh police detectives. The purpose of this profile was to outline the behavioral characteristics of an offender who would commit such murders.

OFFENDER PROFILE
AFFECTIVE/VEHICLE SERIAL KILLER

SEX: *Male*

AGE: 28-35

ETHNICITY: African-American

EMPLOYMENT: *unskilled (e.g., construction worker or cook)*

EDUCATION: *high school dropout*

MARITAL STATUS: *single or divorced*

MILITARY SERVICE:
If he does have a military history, then it will consist of a dishonorable discharge.

ARREST RECORD

The killer will have past convictions of burglary, DWI, reckless driving, and petty crimes. However, this does not reflect the complete criminal record of this killer. In the examiner's opinion the killer will most likely have committed a series of rapes within the same geographical area of where the murders took place. This offender has killed in the past and will continue to kill until caught.

BEHAVIOR

In the examiner's opinion the killer has an explosive personality: he is impulsive, quick-tempered, and self-centered. He is not reclusive but he may have some trouble fitting into the crowd. Generally speaking, however, his social relationships are superficial and limited to drinking buddies and visiting prostitutes.

In the examiner's opinion the killer has conflicts over his relationships with women; he often feels dependent and aggressively resistant to them. While the killer is contested by women, he uses various forms of aggression to get even and degrade them.

Historically, if ever married, his marriage has been ill-fated and he is usually in some phase of estrangement. In the marriage there would have been some history of spousal abuse. The offender will most likely live alone, or among his peers of the same age (e.g., in a hostel). Sexually, he is frustrated and may feel impotent. He links anger with sexual competence. He may use soft pornography but not hardcore pornographic materials for stimulation.

Due to the offender's unpredictable behaviors and aggression, he may have a record of being referred to a mental health worker. He has difficulty with authority figures. In the opinion of the examiner, the killer's crimes will be committed in a stylized violent burst of attack for the purposes of retaliation, or getting even and revenge on women. The victim is used as a vehicle to be exploited. The crime will be unplanned.

The attack on the victims will likely be blitz with heavy trauma to the face. The mildest reaction from the victim can lead to the murder. The crime is an emotional one due to the anger and often results in non-completed sexual acts. The offender will leave evidence scattered about and will show no signs of being forensically aware.

Blunt force trauma on the victims will be present. The offender will use weapons of opportunity such as hands and rocks. Any restraints used will not be brought to the crime scene, but will be of opportunity. If strangulation is indicated, it is likely to be manual. The murder weapon and restraint will likely be found not too far from the crime scene. Victims of this type of killer are usually strangers, but can be acquaintances from the offender's own peer group.

The offender will be relevantly new to the area (less than a year). If there is a series of unsolved rapes in the same vicinity of the murders, then he will mostly have committed the rapes and live in that area. The offender will drive an older (six years older or more) vehicle, but most of his traveling is by foot or public transportation.

To profile the Raleigh murders, I once again used the Predator geopraphical profiling program. The map it generated shows the dump locations of the victims' bodies. The circle indicates the highest probable area (44 percent), where the police should search for the killer. This circular area is roughly one mile in diameter. The star in the lower left-hand corner of the circle, near the victim Ashe, represents my prediction of killer's home base. As shown below, the actual location of John Williams's home was just one block from my predicted location.

My geographical analysis predicted that the killer's place of residency would be closer to where he first encountered his victims, rather than where their bodies were eventually discovered. I said that the killer would live less than 1 1/2 miles from some of the murders and that he would most likely live in the southern part of Raleigh.

Using my profile, the Raleigh police set up their stakeouts in the predicted area. On February 4, 1997, Raleigh police arrested John Williams Jr., age thirty-five. A Raleigh police officer caught Williams when he heard screaming and then choking sounds from inside a parked van in an industrial lot on the 600 block of West Hargett Street. When the cop opened the door, he found Williams in the act of raping a woman, who later identified him through a police line up.

PSYCHO-GEOGRAPHICAL PROFILING MAP OF JOHN WILLIAMS, JR.

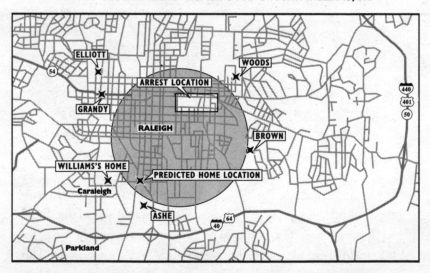

Rectangle indicates area of Williams's arrest while attacking another victim
Circle indicates police search area

As shown on the map, the 600 block of West Hargett Street, represented as a rectangle, is located in my predicted circle. Police were close enough to hear the screams because they had set up extensive stakeouts in the area based on my geographical profile. Williams's home, marked *HB,* was one block from the location I had predicted to be the killer's home base.

Ironically, Williams had been in and out of the hands of Raleigh police since the fall of 1996, when he was arrested on three separate occasions on a variety of charges ranging from robbery and strong-arm robbery right down to resisting arrest and possessing drug paraphernalia. In between bookings, Williams lived in one of Wake County's winter overflow shelters in South Raleigh.

My psychological profile of the unsolved series of murders in Raleigh was accurate on most of the key points. The profile said the killer would be a black man between the ages of twenty-eight and thirty-five; would work an unskilled job, such as that of a cook; would be single or divorced; and would probably live alone or in a hostel or similar place.

John Williams Jr. was black, and at the time of his arrest, thirty-five years-old, turning thirty-six soon thereafter. He was a cook at a Wendy's restaurant across from North Carolina State University. Williams was an unmarried transient relatively new to the city of Raleigh. He lived in South Raleigh in a homeless shelter less than one half mile from where the victims were attacked and murdered, as the profile had suggested.

As also predicted, Williams committed numerous rapes in the same vicinity where the murders occurred. Similarly, Williams had a long criminal record of sexual assaults dating back as far as twenty years in Augusta, Georgia. If Raleigh investigators had relied on my psychological profile early on in the investigation, John Williams Jr. could have been apprehended before additional lives were lost.

On March 31, 1997, Williams was indicted for the first-degree murders of Deborah Jean Elliott and Patricia Ann Ashe, the first-degree rapes of Jacqueline Crump and Audrey Marie Hall, first-degree sexual offense against Audrey Marie Hall, and two counts of assault with a deadly weapon with intent to kill on Jacqueline Crump and Audrey Marie Hall. Williams spent the rest of the year in and out of court being indicted on a variety of rape and assault charges.

Prosecutors Shelley Desvousges and Rebecca Holt built their case on DNA evidence, the surviving victims' identification of Williams in court, and Williams's statement to police after his arrest. DNA tests linked Williams's sperm to Ashe and the two rape victims. A major clue in the case came when Marty Ludas, a latent print examiner for the City-County Bureau of Identification (CCBI), compared the shoeprint lifted from glass pieces from the Elliott crime to John Williams's shoeprints. Ludas formed the opinion that only one shoe could have made that print: John William's left shoe.

No other physical evidence linked Williams to the Ashe slaying, but the rape victims and the three other women who took the witness stand pointed out Williams as their attacker. The women remembered their attacker as "gap-toothed." Ironically, police had had a sketch done earlier in the case from eyewitnesses who claimed the killer was a gap-toothed black man but had ultimately discarded it.

Before the trial began on January 12, 1998, a Raleigh dentist fitted Williams with an upper plate. Still, Williams was compelled several times to remove the denture in court so that witnesses could better identify him.

The evidence would prove to be devastating. The jury found Williams guilty of the two 1996 murders of Patricia Ashe and Deborah Elliott; the first-degree rape of Jacqueline Crump and Audrey Hall; the attempted first degree rape of Shelly Jackson; the assault with a deadly weapon with intent to kill of Shelly Jackson; and other felony charges too numerous to name.

Following a capital sentencing proceeding, the jury recommended a sentence of death for two of the murders. The trial court also sentenced Williams to over two hundred years in prison on the lesser charges. As of October 2004, all of John Williams's appeals have been denied. He remains on death row in North Carolina.

If the Raleigh Police Department had used a linking process like the one previously demonstrated in this chapter, the murders could have been connected earlier, thereby resulting in less money being spent, reduction in man-hours, and most important, lives saved. Thankfully, since the John Williams serial murders, the Raleigh Police Department has taken great strides to improve on its ability to link crimes.

The *News & Observer* later ran a story about my work, headlined "Academic Sleuth Made Startling Predictions." Not so startling, really, if you understand the science behind it. I was honored when the four-term governor of North Carolina, Jim Hunt, later recognized me for my work on the John Williams case.

CHAPTER 4

THE FBi CATCHES
SERiAL KiLLERS . . .

FORGET SILENCE OF THE LAMBS. Serial killers with the panache of Hannibal Lecter do not exist. Neither do FBI profilers like Clarice Starling. That is all the creation of novelist Thomas Harris. Yet, the public believes Harris's vision, that the Bureau's legendary Behavioral Science Section is out there every day protecting us from this most deadly of human predators. Nothing could be further from the truth. That's all it is, a novelist's vision.

The FBI has never caught a serial killer. Not a one. The profiles they turn out on serial killers are closer to Harris's fiction than scientific fact. They are based upon interviews conducted in 1978 with thirty-six convicted killers, out of which only twenty-five were actual serial killers. That FBI "study" has since been condemned as statistically and demographically invalid by one academic after another. But because that condemnation has come from inside the ivy-covered walls of academia, and the police culture refuses to allow a dissenting opinion, the media has ignored the Bureau's sleight-of-hand.

Another dirty little secret in the law enforcement community is that the FBI profiles on serial killers are cookie-cutter. They are always the same: white guy, high school dropout, difficulty with social skills, yada, yada, yada. Jerry Seinfeld could be writing them, or maybe Larry David, that's how dry and lifeless they are. Despite the significant loss of life from the actions of serial killers, and the cost of extended police investigations, a scientific examination to validate FBI profiles has never been carried out.

The myth that the FBI catches serial killers really began with a psychiatrist named James A. Brussel. In 1957, Brussel developed a profile of George Metesky, also known as the "Mad Bomber." It was one of the earliest formal profiles ever done. Brussel subsequently became friends with Howard Teten, a veteran FBI field agent. Teten and Brussels had conversations about the clinical aspects of criminal behavior. This prompted Teten to develop and teach an applied criminology course at the FBI academy in Quantico, Virginia. Teten's course and profiling conversations with Dr. Brussel would eventually lead to the development of the FBI's Behavioral Science Unit, but before that could happen, there had to be "data" on which to base its development.

In the late 1970s, the FBI began a formal project to try to identify the common characteristics of serial murderers and thus to aid in their capture. With good intentions, the FBI proceeded, but unfortunately without scientific evaluation. Between 1978 and 1983, FBI agents conducted a series of interviews with thirty-six incarcerated offenders, only twenty-five of whom were defined as serial murderers. Prior to the interviews, information on the offenders and their crimes was obtained by reviewing everything from crime scene photos to psychiatric reports. Each of the thirty-six was interviewed using an unstructured checklist of questions. When the results were analyzed, the FBI claimed that a simple dichotomy emerged.

Serial killers should be put into two distinct categories, the Bureau argued, organized and disorganized. These categories seem to describe the different levels of aggression in serial murderers, but the FBI profilers never made that clear. The FBI also made no attempt to show that the serial murder project was a scientifically based study. No attempt was made to confirm the findings using different data on serial killers or even serial rapists.

Howard Teten's interests in Dr. Brussels's clinical and motivational approach to profiling helped shape the FBI's organized and disorganized profiling approach. Then came *Red Dragon* and the truth was lost.

Thomas Harris published *Red Dragon,* the first mainstream piece of American fiction to glorify the Behavioral Science Unit, in 1981. The book, a bestseller, introduced the serial killer Hannibal "The Cannibal" Lecter as a supporting character. The film version, 1986's *Manhunter,* was a brilliant evocation of the novel but not a hit with moviegoers. As played by Brian Cox, Lecter was as much slimy as anything else. But Harris knew a good character on the page when he saw one. In *The Silence of the Lambs,* published in 1988, Harris placed Lecter front and center. Lecter's adversary was a rookie FBI agent named Clarice Starling. In the book's film version in 1991, Sir Anthony Hopkins, in a career-defining performance of not more than twenty minutes on screen, made Lecter a cultural icon. But he also did more than just that.

Hopkins made serial killers *accessible.* For the first time, one of them appeared before the public not as some social misfit with the sharply categorized FBI type of behavior, but as a living, breathing, albeit evil human being. He just also happened to have Hopkins's panache, charm, and style. A fictionalized portrayal of a serial killer, sure, but the movie took off. In no small degree was this also due to Jodie Foster's brilliant performance as FBI agent-in-training Clarice Starling. The byplay between these two stars is what made the film a hit, and, by extension, cemented in the public's mind the view that the FBI does indeed track down and capture serial killers. And so the myth continued.

Throughout the eighties and into the nineties and beyond, the FBI publicized its profiling "services" in a number of high-profile cases. For example, in 1983, then-FBI profiler John Douglas examined a letter sent to the Green River Killer task force; he would report that the letter was not from the Green River serial killer. However, we now know that Gary Ridgway, the convicted Green River Killer, did indeed write that letter to the task force. When recently asked about his 1983 analysis of the letter, Douglas denied ever doing an analysis of the letter until a *Seattle Times* reporter provided him the original copy of his analysis on FBI letterhead. Douglas then claimed he remembered, but probably forgot due to his illness back in 1983.

Retired FBI profilers, criminologists, and rogue profilers around the world often step forward to offer their opinions to police investigators or television shows, based on nothing more than their personal experiences in serial killer cases. Take the case of the mailbox pipe bomber, twenty-one-year-old Lucas John Helder. Before Helder was arrested in 2002, former FBI profiler Clint Van Zandt publicly pegged the perpetrator as an older white man with some military experience. It turned out that the suspect, college student Lucas John Helder, wasn't old and had never been in uniform. Van Zandt was right on a few elements: the bomber was single, hailed from a small town, and knew the Midwest. Unfortunately, these inferences were just common sense based on the nature of the crime. Van Zandt's profile played no role in Helder's arrest. He was identified with the help of his father and others who got letters with phrases and antigovernment rants similar to notes the bomber had left in mailboxes throughout the Midwest and West.

In some instances, profilers have talked to various criminals over the years or worked on specific cases; their ideas are determined by what they happened to remember, the cases they happened to have worked on, and the importance they have placed on particular characteristics that they noticed. If you find yourself watching one of these guys deliver their analysis on TV and what they're saying doesn't make sense to you, it isn't that you don't understand. It's that *they* don't. They have about as much chance of profiling a serial killer as Curt Schilling has of winning three hundred games.

For example, during the sniper shootings in the Washington, D.C., area, on-air profilers identified the sniper as a serial killer. Not only did they get that simple point wrong—the snipers were spree killers—there were two snipers, not one. Profilers who missed the mark relied on assumptions about American serial killers—assumptions, not facts. The poison in profiles is reflected in this type of flawed decision making. The psychology of a spree killer is not going to match that of a serial killer. Serial killing and spree killing are different crimes, and in each case development of a truly accurate profile requires a different set of data.

On the television show *CSI* and its various derivations (*CSI's* William S. Petersen played the FBI profiler in *Manhunter*) criminalists profile, wield microscopes, conduct interviews with suspects, and then take time out to qualify on the pistol range. It is, of course, bullshit. Ironically, *CSI* got it right during its first season, when the criminalists were confined to being scientific, but ratings and demographics forced the producers to concede a little more "t and a" and drama would help the ratings. They were right. Marg Helgenberger's T-shirts were tighter than ever and the show was a hit. Profiling, of course, suffered.

There is more to criminal profiling or crime scene investigations than just collecting and analyzing forensic clues left behind by the bad guy. The most important aspect is the method that profilers rely on for their decision making, specifically what they use to draw inferences between behaviors at the crime scene and the type of offender police are looking for. Too many profiling consultants to the police draw their template from fictional models rather than scientific ones. And if they do rely on "science," it is the antiquated, rickety, someone-should-have-left-it-for-dead-a-long-time-ago FBI serial killer "study."

Offender profiling has developed into a field where scientific processes have been ignored in favor of quick answers based on specious experience. To make a judgment for a single event based on probability like "75 percent of serial killers do this" is the argument that some profilers use to suggest that the FBI's method of profiling is inductive rather than deductive. To use this analogy shows a lack of knowledge and a misrepresentation of the FBI profiling model.

FBI profilers have always sat around a table at Quantico, Virginia, reviewing the facts of a case and brainstorming about the personality of the offender who committed the crime in question. This "gut feeling" process is deductive rather than inductive. Furthermore, the FBI's organized and disorganized typology was developed using limited data on serial killers. What descriptive probabilities in the organized and disorganized model do FBI profilers draw on for crimes like rape and arson? None. Yet profilers from all over the world use the organized and disorganized typology to profile various crimes.

Consider this: in the FBI's 1978 serial murder project, more disorganized killers participated in the interviews than organized killers. That should mean that if FBI profilers were continually relying on percentage probabilities to develop profiles, then their profiles should be skewed toward disorganized offenders.

The FBI's organized and disorganized model is the most widely used profiling model in the world. Profilers who rely on this approach don't refer back to those journal articles to see what percentage of serial killers performed what act. The crime scene actions that define the organized and disorganized typology were not chosen based on descriptive percentages and neither are their profiles.

Rather than pulling conclusions out of thin air like deductive profilers, I justify my profiling conclusions with the Law of Large Numbers. Admittedly, I don't know the true probability, due to our finite existence, given such a large number of cases; I can approximate the actual probability. I don't have to know everything to know something. Also, I don't have to know every case to get an approximation. This approximation is sufficient to fix my beliefs and lead to further inquiry in a case. I apply abduction, deduction, and induction together to achieve a comprehensive inquiry. This is a scientific approach to crime analysis and profiling.

For sure, the scientific approach to profiling is like a revolving door; as new data is added our results are refined to make it more applicable and accurate. In short, abduction creates, deduction explicates, and induction verifies. Relying solely on abduction or deductive logic, profilers are avoiding the most crucial aspect of a scientific foundation for criminal profiling; that is, providing a scientific basis for their conclusions rather than just relying on mere hunches, brainstorming, work experience, and gut feelings.

Only proper data collection and thorough research can bring credibility to profiling. When police collect forensic evidence at a crime scene, they should be collecting the information to solve future crimes, not just the one in question. Currently, there are no professional standards or licensing requirements for this line of work. When self-proclaimed profilers repeat the same terminology as qualified profilers, detectives, the media, and the public believe them.

For example, my research on five hundred-plus serial murder cases shows that most serial killers are not clever at alluding police; they get caught through their own mistakes or a tip from the public. My work has also found that serial killers are consistent in their behaviors over time. These conclusions challenge cherished myths, myths that many have exploited for ill-gotten gain by charlatans masquerading as scientific profilers. What is really sad is how many in the media and law enforcement believe them, and how many lives are lost as a result.

Task forces and detectives that have relied on the FBI's profilers have been plagued by inaccurate profiles. For example, FBI profilers were way off the mark in their predictions in the Unabomber case, as shown in the profile below:

FBI PROFILE	TED KACZYNSKI
Late 30's or early 40's	Kaczynski was 53 when arrested
White Male, 5' 10" – 6' tall, 165 pounds, with reddish-blond hair, a thin mustache and a ruddy complexion	Kaczynski is 5'8", weighed 143 when arrested, with brown hair, bearded and pale skin. He was, however, a white male; so is half the country.
A blue collar worker with a high school diploma	Kaczynski hadn't had a job in the last 25 years and has a Ph.D. in mathematics from the University of Michigan in addition to being a graduate of Harvard University.
A meticulously organized person, reclusive and having problems dealing with women	Kaczynski was a recluse who apparently did not deal with women at all and he was slovenly and unkempt. He was however a recluse; so was Howard Hughes.

Even a number of FBI agents remain skeptical of their own profiling process due to the potential for profiles to mislead investigators. In fact, one of the FBI's well-known profilers, Robert Ressler, stated in a 1983 interview that he was responsible for producing the most inaccurate profile in the agency's history. However, his confession may have been the last time an FBI profiler admitted to being wrong. Take the case of Henry Louis Wallace, who had raped and murdered nine women in Charlotte, North Carolina.

After the first five murders, Wallace was arrested for shoplifting in a mall, and although his name was found in the address books of several of the deceased women, he was released from custody. Why? Because FBI profilers had assured the Charlotte police that the murders were not the work of a serial killer. There were, actually, a multitude of similarities among the murders: the victims were young, attractive, African-American women killed in their homes, all with evidence of ligature strangulation. All the women had been killed within a five-mile radius. There were some differences among the murders. For example, one woman was stabbed to death after she proved too difficult to strangle, one was set on fire after being strangled. Still, you'd expect that any self-trained profiler could have pegged the rash of deaths as the work of a serial killer. But that did not happen in this case.

The FBI profilers convinced local law enforcement that the deaths were all unrelated. Wallace went on to murder four more women before being arrested and confessing to all nine counts. At Wallace's trial, Robert Ressler said, "If [Henry Louis Wallace] elected to become a serial killer, he was going about it the wrong way." That's because most serial killers are Caucasian, but Wallace was African-American; most serial killers murder strangers, but Wallace knew all of his victims. What all of this means, of course, is that the profilers had been wrong, so far off-the-deep-end wrong that they felt the need to actually blame the serial killer for not looking like what they had expected to find. On January 29, 1997, Wallace was given the death sentence. He currently is on death row in Raleigh, North Carolina. The FBI not only fumbled the ball, they blew the game, and the price was innocent people's lives.

If I had profiled the Wallace case, my analysis would have likely pegged the killer. My research on serial killers who entered their victims' homes found that the offenders are more likely to be black. In the Wallace case, and as we shall see in the case of the Baton Rouge Serial Killer, everyone but me profiled the offender as white. Perhaps that's because there is an inherent bias in the FBI profile to stay away from defining African-Americans as serial criminals. Yes, about 16 percent of serial killers are African-American, but in the FBI model, it's as if African-Americans don't exist at all.

Still another theory to explain criminal behavior is environmental criminology. Drs. Brantingham and Brantingham coined the phrase in the late 1970s. Environmental criminology is concerned with criminal mobility and the relationship between offenders' home bases and their target areas. Environmental criminology attempts to outline a theoretical geographical area that an offender will victimize, based not on demographic features but on the individual's own mental image of the area.

The Brantinghams proposed a theoretical spatial model for looking at journeys to crime as they occur in urban space. The Brantinghams' model uses concepts of opportunity and offender motivation together with the concepts of mobility and perception to predict the next likely target area and the offender's residence. However, to my knowledge, their theories have never been scientifically verified.

In later research, the Brantinghams expanded their model using theoretical cases. The simplest case scenario, and subsequently the foundation for Dr. Kim Rossmo's geographical profiling system, is the basic search area for an individual offender. Their first hypothesized search area involved a single offender, uniform distribution of potential targets, and the offender living in a single location.

The Brantinghams borrowed from decays of spatial research on distance decay models in describing the location of an offender's crimes. Distance decay refers to the reduction of activity or interaction as distance from the home increases. In their second model, the Brantinghams hypothesized that the expected range of a criminal would be circular and that most offenses would occur close to home, with the likelihood of an offense taking place in a particular location decreasing with distance from home.

They suggested offenders would have more cognized mental maps about potential crime opportunities close to their home bases. They also proposed that offenders would be more likely to be noticed and identified close to their home bases by other individuals who live in the same vicinity. They argued that there would be a "confront zone" directly around the offender's home base where little criminal activity would occur, which is referred to as a "buffer zone."

This implies that it takes effort, time, and money to overcome distance; these things are referred to as the "friction of distance." In later research, the Brantinghams refined their hypothesized spatial model and proposed a complex search area for offenders. The initial conditions allows for the fact that criminals, like noncriminals, are not tied only to geographical locations near their home base. Rather, offenders, like nonoffenders, go to work, shop, and relax, and the pathways between all these activities combine to form what they termed the individual's "awareness space."

The Brantinghams' hypothesized spatial theories suggest that, given equally distributed opportunities, offenders will tend to offend within a minimum and maximum range of distance from the offender's home, independent of direction and other physical or psychological constraints. Their theory, however, has been met with mixed results.

A study found that in Cleveland, Ohio, property offenders tended to travel further from home than personal offenders did. Another study in 1982 found that bank robbers but not burglars traveled longer distances to their crime sites. There have been, however, exceptions to these findings. Consider a study in 1955 that showed that between the years 1945 and 1949, 40 percent of all Houston homicides, including domestic homicides, occurred within one city block of the offenders' residences. At the very least there are some doubts about the validity of the Brantinghams' spatial theories.

Following on the work of the Brantinghams, Dr. Kim Rossmo, calling his technique criminal geographical targeting (CGT), has combined concepts from environmental criminology with a mathematical model, based on a distance decay function, and derived from the locations in which killers leave their victims' bodies, to indicate the area in which an offender may be living. Rossmo's work has suggested that victims are probably spatially biased toward the offender's home base. This theory was illustrated in a study by the Brantinghams in 1981 in Washington, D.C., where they found that offenders generally victimized areas they know best, concentrating on targets within their immediate environments and surrounding areas. This spatial bias is the proposed cause of a decay function such that the further an offender is from home the less likely he is to commit an offense.

The reasons for the decay proposed in Rossmo's criminal geographical targeting model has never been clearly explained but appear to be based on the *least-effort principle*. The least-effort principle says that when multiple destinations of equal desirability are available, all else being equal, the closest one will be chosen.

Rossmo incorporates another principle into his geographical profiling system that has been put forward as a basis for crime locations:

that there will be a tendency for serial killers to avoid committing crimes close to where they live, aka the *buffer zone*. The proposed reason for this buffer zone is that criminals will avoid leaving incriminating evidence near where they live.

However, a geographical profile dependent on this theory may be limited and misleading, because a buffer zone is not always present. In a 1995 study on single rapists in London, researchers found no evidence for a buffer zone. Another drawback to relying on the distance decay theory is that the actual distances proposed as buffer zones are often larger than would be consistent with leaving local clues. How large is a normal buffer zone—one-half mile, two miles? No specific distance has ever been articulated.

I believe the theories that Rossmo's geographical profiling system is built on are logically in conflict. The same is true for Ned Levine's CrimeStat mapping program produced under a U.S. National Institute of Justice grant. On one hand they argue that there is a tendency to minimize effort close to home, which would predict that crimes are in a closely circumscribed area. On the other hand, there's the tendency for serial killers to keep a minimum distance away from home. I argue that these two processes combined would lead to the prediction of an optimum distance from home for all of a particular type of offense.

The main point is, the general finding is one of an aggregate decay of the frequency of crimes as their distances increase from home. These processes are derived from a consideration of instrumental crimes (means-to-an-end crimes) often with a tangible or material benefit, such as theft, robbery, or rape. I'm not saying that these theories do not have relevance to geographical profiling—they do in some respect—but there are questions about how important emotional issues are, which are ignored in Rossmo's and Levine's profiling models.

CHAPTER 5

. . . AND OTHER LiES

THE PHILOSOPHY OF CRIMINAL profiling in its present form is flawed due to inferred deductive assumptions and leap in the dark conclusions made about offender actions and characteristics, based solely on gut feelings derived from work experience. Consequently, this leads to profiles being unsound and misleading for police investigations. That means more serial killers operating on the street with relative impunity.

The FBI rarely, if ever, releases its profiles, even after a case is solved. As such, we are left with the biased opinions of a selected few about the accuracy of FBI profiles. What has been a poor substitute for profiling accuracy are detectives' claims that they are satisfied with the FBI profiler's advice that they have received, regardless of how accurate the profile actually turned out to be.

FBI profilers were working about five hundred cases a year in 1985, and approximately a thousand a year by 1996. I know of no case in which an FBI profile directly led to the arrest of a serial killer. Of course, it is inevitable that FBI profilers would produce a certain number of reasonably accurate profiles due to the volume of cases alone. Given enough chances at throwing darts at balloons, anyone will eventually bust a few once in a while.

It is important to understand that what the profiling sleuths have to offer these days is a storyline. Novelists lay out a narrative that eventually explains the drama as well as resolving it, which is why psychologists are now so attracted to fictional crime authors. They offer a new set of narrative forms. Motives such as greed, or a despondent wife who conspires to murder her husband over jealousy and revenge, can be replaced with sadistic sexual desires, distorted, displaced relationships, or searches for lost mother figures. It is exactly here where the danger in profiling lies. Motives are complex.

The danger is trying to predict motive from assumptions made about crime scene behavior. Relying on gut feelings and hunches, FBI profilers invent sexy narratives that are often more seductive to detectives than the mere interpretation of clues that a psycho-geographic profiler can provide. Motive somehow provides a whole framework and context within which to consider a set of jumbled facts.

Police investigators are particularly vulnerable to the creative fictions of FBI profilers, because their main task is very similar to that of a fictional crime author. Profilers feel the need to invent a narrative that makes sense of all the facts while at the same time indicating the processes that give the plot its dynamics, usually rather ambiguously referred to as the "motive." One example where the FBI focused on motive to the detriment of the investigation was the explosion aboard the USS *Iowa* in 1989.

The FBI developed a psychological autopsy (profile) of Gunner's Mate Clayton Hartwig, a suspect at that time in the explosion that killed him and forty-six of his shipmates. A bureau analysis requested by the U.S. Navy indicated that Hartwig was suicidal and homicidal. The official supposition was that Hartwig snapped and deliberately set the explosion.

However, the American Psychological Association examined the case more thoroughly, and they established that the FBI's profile was invalid; the wrong methodology was used. Further, hard evidence was discovered that suggested that the explosion was actually accidental. A panel of psychologists and psychiatrists consulted by a U.S. congressional committee looking into the explosion concluded that though it may be tempting to make inferences from crime scene details on the basis of experience, there are a number of considerations that may bias and distort the conclusions. The Navy later withdrew its accusation against Mr. Hartwig, and his reputation in death was saved from an FBI smear based on voodoo profiling.

Profilers try to give us the who, what, and why in their profiles. I believe the why, motive, is often not clear in violent crimes such as serial murder and rape.

FBI profilers actually work backward; they try to answer the why first from the "what'" (crime scene actions) to give them the "who" without any consideration given to the victim and offender interactions in a crime. The FBI profilers' assumption is that a person's primary traits will remain stable. They believe that a person's inclination is to act consistently in a particular way, consistently, across a variety of situations. However, traits are not directly observable but rather are inferred from behavior. I believe that it seems more reasonable to consider crime scene actions as experiences of *behavior* rather than particular manifestations of intrinsic motive.

For example, many profilers deductively conclude that if a murder is particularly violent, the offender must be particularly aggressive. This premise also leads to another conclusion: aggressive offenders commit any given crime in a particularly violent way. What this suggests is that traits are both inferred from and explained by behavior. These examples serve to show how misleading conclusions can be when they depend on this kind of specious, circular reasoning.

An example of circular reasoning is the profile prepared for the Metropolitan Toronto Police by FBI profilers Gregg McCrary and James Wright in the Scarborough rapist case, in which serial killer Paul Bernardo would later be implicated and convicted.

At the time, McCrary and Wright claimed that in observing the first eight offenses of the unknown rapist, the offender could be classified as a "sexual sadist." This led the profilers to conclude that the following characteristics could be predicted on the basis of such a classification system:

- WHITE MALE
- PARENTAL INFIDELITY OR DIVORCE
- MARRIED AT THE TIME OF THE OFFENSE
- KNOWN CROSS-DRESSER
- MILITARY EXPERIENCE
- FASCINATION WITH POLICE WORK

The assumption of FBI profilers is that the amount of chaos at a crime scene is a reflection of the attacker's personality. This deductive profiling mind-set can be seen in a quote from FBI profiler John Douglas in 1992 in which he stated that "the crime scene is presumed to reflect the murderer's behavior and personality in much the same way as furnishings reveal the homeowner's character."

The weakness in this profiling approach is that for the more than two hundred classification categories of murder, rape, and arson that John Douglas and Robert Ressler outlined in their FBI Crime Classification Manual, there have been no systematic efforts to validate these profile-derived classifications. Yet, their profiling derivations continue to enjoy a consistent presence in the literature.

The FBI is still asked routinely to consult on serial murder investigations, despite the fact that FBI profilers' opinions are often rejected on appeals, as demonstrated in the following murder cases.

COMMONWEALTH OF PENNSYLVANIA V. DISTEFANO

In 1999, a Common Pleas Court judge ruled that profiling testimony wasn't permissible in Pennsylvania because it wasn't based on sound scientific principles. No surprise there. What was surprising for a lot of people was that the profiler in question was Roy Hazelwood—one of the FBI's former profiling pioneers.

The defense attorney in the case claimed that Mr. Hazelwood's profiling testimony was "speculative and expressed in terms of probabilities . . . [with] little probative value." The attorney also equated FBI profiling techniques to "voodoo," and said that profilers were ". . . just glorified mystics." The judge not only agreed but ruled that Mr. Hazelwood could not discuss anything regarding the behavioral traits of a typical murderer, or specific characteristics or behavior of the defendant. In other words, it wasn't fair to say something like, "Killers usually watch slasher movies and read pornography, therefore it is likely that he is a killer."

THE STEVEN FORTIN MURDER CASE

On August 11, 1994, twenty-five-year-old Melissa Padilla was living in a room at the Gem Motel in Woodbridge, New Jersey, with her four children, ages two to five, and her boyfriend, Hector Fernandez. To earn extra money, they dealt small amounts of drugs out of their motel room. Sometime around 11:00 P.M., Padilla went down to the motel office to use the pay phone to order pizza. She had trouble getting the pizza place on the phone and set out to buy food at a local convenience store about 350 yards north along Route 1, at the corner of Avenel Street.

Midnight came and went. Fernandez began to worry about Padilla and decided to go look for her. He left the children in the room and went to the front desk to ask Addie Lawrence, the night clerk, if she had seen her. Lawrence told him that she had seen Padilla trying to phone for a pizza, but that she had been unsuccessful and had left, walking toward the Quik Chek convenience store.

Trent Eubanks, a friend of Fernandez's, who had driven him to New York earlier in the day to buy marijuana, was also in the motel office. Fernandez asked Eubanks to help him look for Padilla. They both walked all the way to the Quik Chek, passing in front of the Americana Motel and the Premium Diner, across Wiley Street. They continued walking along the dirt path in front of the vacant lot that was the site of a construction project, past the Avenel Motel and across Avenel Street, finally reaching the convenience store. Padilla was still nowhere in sight.

Fernandez and Eubanks returned to the Gem Motel. Eubanks offered to drive Hector around to look for Padilla, if he could get his car started. His car had broken down at the end of the New York trip and he had left it sitting on Wiley Street. Eubanks borrowed the battery from Lawrence's car and went to try to start his car. Meanwhile, Fernandez again started out along the path to the Quik Chek. Walking past a vacant construction site just north of Wiley Street, he noticed a couple of plastic grocery bags near the south side of four eight-foot-long, thirty-inch-diameter sewer pipes that were on the ground awaiting installation. The pipes were lying next to each other, perpendicular to Route 1, about ten feet from the roadway. The bags were on the ground a few feet from the pipes. New-looking food items were strewn on the ground. Fernandez hurriedly walked over and bent down to inspect the food. It was there that he found Padilla.

Padilla's feet were sticking out the of east end of the northernmost pipe. Covered in blood, naked from the waist down, she was motionless and silent. Heart racing, Fernandez pulled Padilla out of the pipe and began yelling at her to wake up. Pounding on her chest, he got no response. He began yelling for Eubanks, who was not far away on Wiley Street attempting to get his car cranked.

Eubanks heard him yelling and ran over. After seeing Padilla's lifeless body, Eubanks ran back to the Gem Motel to call the police. The dispatch call went out over the police radio at 12:55 A.M. By that time, Eubanks had run back to what was now a crime scene. Seeing the children from the motel starting to walk over toward the body, Eubanks took his T-shirt off and gave it to Fernandez, who used it to cover Padilla's lower torso.

The first policeman on the scene was Officer Michael Dalia. Officer Dalia approached Eubanks and Fernandez, who was still very excited. Fernandez pointed out Padilla's body. Officer Dalia checked her vital signs, determining that she was dead, then turned his attention to securing the crime scene as a crowd started to gather.

Other officers began to arrive. In all, there were fourteen officers on scene when the lead homicide investigator Detective Sergeant Lawrence Nagle arrived at 1:22 A.M. The evidence control officer, Investigator James O'Brien, had already started his crime scene examination, observing evidence in place. Fernandez was taken back to the motel and allowed to make arrangements for Padilla's children. For a brief moment, Eubanks spoke to the police, but then went to his room and was not transported to the police station to give a formal statement until a few hours later.

Finally, at approximately 2:07 A.M., the Middlesex County Medical Examiner, Dr. Marvin Shuster, arrived and did his on-site examination before transporting the body to the morgue for autopsy. As a precaution, Dr. Shuster took a vaginal swab of the victim at the scene, probably so that evidence would not be rubbed off in transit.

The autopsy later documented in graphic detail what was generally apparent as Padilla lay on the ground that night. She had been brutally beaten about her upper face. Blood covered her face, hair, and the front of her shirt. Her eyes and forehead were black and blue and swollen, her nose was broken, and there were lacerations and abrasions on her face. There was no doubt that she had endured a severe beating. There were bruises on her neck, and the hyoid bone was fractured, which was indicative of strangulation. There were numerous areas of internal hemorrhage in the neck tissues. There were also abrasions on the front and back of her knees and lower legs.

The medical examiner observed other marks on Padilla's chin and her left breast, a few of which he thought had the appearance of possible bite marks. Dr. Jay Kartagener, a dentist, concluded that they were probably bite marks, confirming Dr. Shuster's suspicions. Dr. Shuster also found evidence of sexual assault, both vaginal and anal, but the killer left little semen. He concluded that Padilla's death was the result of assault and strangulation resulting in asphyxiation.

In the days and weeks following the discovery of Padilla's body, the detectives assigned to the case investigated a variety of suspects, but leads petered out. It was obvious that Padilla encountered her attacker after leaving the store with her groceries. The killer, who had gone for a quick kill, most likely encountered Padilla about ten feet off the path, just south of the four sewer pipes, because that is where her groceries were found. From the initial encounter site, the assault appeared to move down the path near to where her sandals were found—near the sewer pipes. It was odd that there was not much blood outside the pipe, so Padilla had to have been moved pretty far from the point of attack, fairly quickly.

The murder could have been the work of a lone killer or possibly two. The attack location suggested a single attacker, though, because it occurred mainly in the pipe, where there was barely room for one person. Maybe there had been someone else acting as a lookout?

It was unclear how many persons were involved in the murder. It was unclear if she had known her assailant(s). It was unclear if the reason for the initial contact was a robbery, or sexual motives, or if it was triggered by some verbal interchange with the victim.

Whatever or whomever, Melissa Padilla's murder was strange.

The killer had beaten her face viciously, apparently with his fists, stuffed her in the pipe, beaten her some more, strangled her, ripped off her pants, apparently bit her on the breast and chin, apparently inserted an object in her anus, stolen her jewelry, then walked off toward Wiley Street covered in blood, carrying her shorts and panties in one hand and one of her sandwiches from her recent grocery purchase in the other.

The killer had then tossed Padilla's shorts and panties into a tall bush on Wiley Street, taken a bite out of the sandwich and left it sitting on a fence on the corner of Wiley and Jansen Avenue, and ambled off into the night. No one saw a thing even though the neighborhood was full of people. Still, the attack didn't surprise those who lived nearby—transients were common in the area.

A search of the immediate crime scene area produced some evidence. Crime scene technicians picked up a smoked cigarette from the west end of one sewer pipe. There was no telling how long it had been there though. Maybe detectives would find new clues, or maybe she had hurt the guy and blood would be recovered. The bite marks on her breast and chin, assuming they were actually bite marks, would provide forensic clues. The ME hadn't seemed that sure to begin with.

If there were ever any forensic results, there were plenty of guys to compare them to. There was Padilla's boyfriend Fernandez, his friend Eubanks, and some transients in the vicinity that the detectives had interviewed. But they didn't really feel strongly about any of them. Most did not seem very violent, though there were some with violent attacks in their background. All had cooperated—no one had requested their constitutional right to a lawyer. Most could account for the time of the murder fairly persuasively, all voluntarily gave blood and hair samples, and most took and passed police polygraphs. There wasn't much to go on. Investigators waited for the results from the state police lab. When they came in, the results weren't very helpful either.

Whoever smoked the cigarette was a secretor with blood type A, but it still was not clear that the cigarette was connected to the crime. About eighty percent of humans are secretors, meaning that their blood can be typed based on body fluids such as salvia or feces. But no other blood type except the victim's was found. No fiber evidence had been turned up on her body or clothes. All of the pubic hair and all the head hair found had been hers, so far as anybody could prove, with just two exceptions. These were a pubic hair found on her stomach, and a short brown head hair. The head hair could have come from almost anywhere. Without DNA, single hairs didn't yield very strong evidence anyway. The pubic hair looked potentially helpful. But when it was compared to the suspects, there were no matches. The evidence was not only too weak to convict; they still didn't have a viable suspect.

A forensic odontologist could look at the bite marks and the suspect's teeth, but that was expensive. Besides, detectives really didn't think any of those interviewed so far was the killer. Maybe DNA might help, they thought. It wasn't until January of 1995, after the state lab had finished all the forensic analysis that it could do, that the various swabs and the cigarette were submitted for DNA testing to Cellmark, Inc., a leading private DNA identification laboratory.

The DNA submissions were incomplete. The cops didn't even bother to test samples from most of the suspects, just Fernandez, and they didn't expect anything from that. They got what they expected. In fact, the report that came back from Cellmark in March looked potentially to be less helpful than usual.

Most of the forensic evidence seemed to be the victim's DNA. What wasn't hers had glitches with various control tests, and a lot of the samples may or may not have been mixtures, which can create real problems. Investigators were at a dead end. No suspects, no leads, no nothing.

On April 11, 1995. Lt. Lawrence Nagle of the Middlesex County Major Crimes Unit picked up the phone. He was the original lead detective in charge of the Melissa Padilla murder investigation. The call was from Detective Theodos of the New Jersey State Police Major Crimes Unit. New Jersey State Police had received a call earlier from the Maine State Police asking them to do a background investigation on a Steven Fortin, age thirty, who had been arrested in Maine for an April 3 attack on a female Maine state trooper during a routine traffic stop. Fortin had given Woodbridge, New Jersey, as his most recent home address.

Fortin was a violent individual. Without warning, he had repeatedly punched off-duty state trooper Vicki Gardner in the face, attempted to strangle her with his hands, pulled off her sweatpants, and sexually assaulted her with his hands, both vaginally and anally. Notably, he bit her on the breast and chin.

As Nagle listened to the story about Fortin the hairs curled on his neck—Fortin's attack on the state trooper and some of the behavior in the Padilla murder were similar. The more he heard, the more he knew that this just might be the lead he'd been waiting for to solve this open murder.

Dawn Quinn, whom Fortin had identified as his girlfriend,

confirmed Nagle's assumptions, placing Fortin, drunk and angry, within two hundred yards of the Padilla murder scene a little over an hour before Padilla was killed. A criminal records check revealed that Fortin had spent seven years in prison for the stabbing death of his own brother. Steven Fortin became the number one suspect in the murder of Melissa Padilla.

In her interview with police, Quinn said that she was twenty-eight years old when she met Steven Fortin through friends in April of 1994. They had moved in together soon after meeting. In August of 1994, Quinn and Fortin were living at the Douglas Motel, which was just down the road north of the Quik Chek convenience store on Route 1. Fortin was working for a paving contractor; she was unemployed.

On a warm night in early August 1994, Quinn and Fortin left their motel and walked south on Route 1 to the Quik Chek convenience store, where they purchased cigarettes. They then walked south, past the construction site and the Gem Motel, then past a bar and restaurant called Bud's Hut, finally arriving at the Five Oaks apartments, which was across Tappen Street from Bud's Hut on Route 1. They had gone to the Five Oaks to visit Quinn's friend, Bruce Beane.

The two arrived around 9:00 P.M. and spent the next hour and a half drinking with Beane at the Five Oaks. Quinn and Fortin got drunk and began to argue over their relationship. Still loaded, they left Beane's place a little before 10:30 P.M. and walked through the parking lot of Bud's Hut; their argument escalated. Fortin knocked Quinn down. He jumped on her but she got loose and ran into Bud's Hut and called the police. The call was received at dispatch around 10:32 P.M. When the police arrived minutes later, Fortin was gone.

Quinn was drunk and belligerent, but she did have bruises and a bloody nose. She told the police her story and said that she wanted to press charges against Fortin, and then refused to swear out a formal complaint. Quinn went to the hospital in an ambulance, but refused to be treated.

Instead, she walked to her mother's house in nearby Perth Amboy and did not see Fortin again until two days later on Saturday. He then talked her into moving back in with him. They stayed together in the area until late December, when they went to Maine to visit his parents. Late in January 1995, they traveled back to New Jersey, stopping to visit her father in Connecticut. During the stopover they had another fight in which she received a black eye. Fortin left and she did not see him again after that.

On April 12, Nagle called the Maine authorities to get more details on the Maine charges. On learning the full details of Fortin's attack on Trooper Gardner in Maine, Nagle's experience told him that Fortin could be good for the Padilla murder. The Maine authorities told Nagle that Fortin had agreed to a plea deal on the Maine charges. Still in custody, impressions were made of his teeth for comparison to Trooper Gardner's bite wounds just in case he reneged on his plea and went to trial. That evidence could also be used if he was ever charged with Padilla's murder.

The teeth impressions were sent to Dr. Lowell Levine, a leading forensic odontologist and bite mark identification expert. But because of the plea agreement, he didn't really make any comparisons with the photographs of the Gardner bite wounds. Nagle directed that Levine be contacted by the New Jersey detectives and be provided with the autopsy report and other details of the Padilla case, including photographs of Melissa Padilla's bite wounds. Dr. Levine was then asked to compare the casts of Fortin's teeth previously provided by the Maine authorities with Melissa Padilla's bite wounds.

On May 3, Levine issued a report that positively identified Steven Fortin's teeth as the source of the bite wounds on Melissa Padilla's left breast.

Nagle went up to Maine on April 24 to attempt to take a statement from Fortin. Fortin did not request a lawyer but the closest thing he came to admitting the murder was when he was told his teeth had been matched to the bite marks, he replied, "Well, if the evidence says I did it, I must have done it, I don't remember." Unfortunately, when it came back, the DNA evidence was inconclusive. They would need something else to convict Fortin, but that didn't mean he couldn't be charged.

Steven Fortin was indicted for Melissa Padilla's murder in early September 1995, but his incarceration in Maine caused his case to fall into a kind of limbo. It was not until March 1997 that things had progressed to the point that a notice of aggravating factors was filed, the procedure for seeking the death penalty in New Jersey. In the meantime, the District Attorney had a lot of time to mull over his case.

The prosecutor's most powerful evidence in the Padilla murder was the evidence of the details of Fortin's attack on Trooper Gardner in Maine. If the judge allowed in the evidence of the Maine to the jury, Fortin would surely be convicted. If it was not admitted, Fortin might go free. The DA subsequently hired the Academy Group, Inc., to help him win the case.

The Academy Group is a consulting firm comprised of retired criminal profilers from the FBI. One of these profilers was Roy Hazelwood. In August 1997, Mr. Hazelwood agreed to review the Melissa Padilla and Vicki Gardner cases in order to form an expert opinion as to whether the two crimes were committed by the same offender.

The prosecutor wasn't asking Hazelwood for a criminal profile of the killer of Melissa Padilla. Rather, he wanted to know if Hazelwood thought he could offer an expert opinion on whether the Gardner offense—which Fortin had admitted to committing—was committed by the same person as the Padilla murder. In the prosecutor's mind, Hazelwood could make this determination better than the jurors alone could.

Hazelwood's job was basically to determine if there were behavioral similarities between Padilla's murder and the Gardner assault. Did Steven Fortin commit both of the crimes? Hazelwood told the prosecutor yes. To support his claim, Hazelwood invoked a theory to which he attached the name "linkage analysis." Linkage analysis is not a new term and is really no different from traditional profiling. Linkage analysis is also called criminal investigative analysis, behavioral profiling, or just simply criminal profiling.

The process undertaken by Hazelwood was perhaps the ultimate example of confirmatory biased profiling. Hazelwood knew from the outset what was desired by the DA and set about to see if he could deliver it. He also knew from the case information supplied to him by the prosecutor which information was irrelevant, and that there was forensic evidence such as bite mark comparisons that pointed to Fortin's guilt, independent of the details of the two crimes he was to examine for linkage.

Hazelwood was confident of his analysis that, based on the similarities, the same person had committed both crimes. Relying on profiler John Douglas's previous writings on linkage analysis, Hazelwood stated in his report to the prosecution:

When examining crimes for linkage, one must study the offender's behavior for similarities over the crimes. This behavior is referred to as "M.O." (modus operandi) and "Ritualistic" ("Signature") behavior. The M.O. is learned behavior and is developed by the criminal to accomplish three things: Ensure success; Protect identity and; Facilitate escape. Because it is learned behavior, I believe instead that the M.O. is in a constant state of evolution, which allows it to meet the demands of the crimes. Therefore, the M.O. is subject to change over time. The primary causes of these changes are experience, maturity, education. My opinion is the M.O. of the crimes involving Ms. Padilla and Ms. Gardner demonstrate the following similarities:

MELISSA PADILLA'S CRIME	VICKI GARDNER'S CRIME
High-risk crime	High-risk crime
Crime committed impulsively	Crime committed impulsively
Female victim	Female victim
25 years-old	34 years-old
Victim crossed path of offender	Victim crossed path of offender
Assault at confrontation point	Assault at confrontation point
Adjacent to well-traveled roadway	On well-traveled roadway
Occurred during darkness (11:30 P.M.)	Occurred during darkness (8:40 P.M.)
No weapons involved in assault	No weapons involved in assault
Blunt force (fists) injuries	Blunt force (fists) injuries
Trauma primarily to upper face no damage to teeth	Trauma primarily to upper face no damage to teeth
Lower garments totally removed	Lower garments totally removed
Shirt left on victim and breasts free	Shirt left on victim and breasts free
No seminal fluid found on/in victim	No seminal fluid found on/in victim
No theft of valuables	No theft of valuables

The similarities between the two crimes proposed by Hazelwood in the table merely give an illusion of a relationship greater than that which actually existed. Hazelwood's linkage analysis in the Fortin case confirms the finding of a study published in 2003 by former PhD colleagues of mine in the investigative psychology department at Liverpool University. They looked at 3,090 distinct statements made during twenty-one original criminal profiles, including those made by the FBI profilers.

What the researchers found was that most profiles are little better than a horoscope or a reading from a psychic in revealing important information. More than 70 percent of the profile statements studied were simple repetition of facts already known by the police, such as, "The offender wears a size 11 shoe," when an imprint of a size 11 shoe was found at the scene.

More than half of the remaining statements were unverifiable —that is, there would be no way to prove or disprove them, even if the suspect were caught. For example, "The offender holds repressed rage against women." Because there is no way to prove or disprove repressed rage, this is throwaway line designed more for emotional impact than for moving the investigation forward. It helps no one.

The jury in the Fortin case didn't know any of this. Hazelwood made a persuasive witness and Fortin was convicted of murder. But Fortin appealed, and Roy Hazelwood lost another battle. The New Jersey Supreme Court ruled that Hazelwood's use of "linkage analysis" was inadmissible. The problem was that Hazelwood's profile used to link the two attacks, which resulted in Fortin's conviction, was not valid.

In the trial, Hazelwood testified about ritualistic behavior and modus operandi (MO), and offered his opinion that the two assaults were so similar that they had to have been committed by the same person. For example, both women suffered bite marks to the left breast and had their faces beaten severely. Both had been anally raped with an object. Linkage analysis suggests that if two or more crimes have enough commonalities, or links, then it is likely that the same person committed all the crimes.

There was other circumstantial evidence that also connected Fortin to the Padilla murder, but the court ruled that linkage analysis is not a science. There are no guidelines regarding which commonalities might be the most important, how many links are necessary to be sufficient to charge a person with the crimes, or even which dissimilar features might negate a link. There are no scientific "laws of linkage" that would allow all profilers to come to the same conclusion. This is why I insist that only through research will profiling improve. There's no consistency in opinions.

As explained by Hazelwood, such linking of crimes is based on training, education, and experience, not any quantified set of rules. Of course, this lack of rules means that training and education might differ from place to place, profiler to profiler. Depending on the skill and experience of the expert, profiles might vary in terms of degree of sophistication, accuracy, and completeness, but they should at least be based on the same general principles.

The Superior Court found that Hazelwood was indeed an expert in the area of criminal investigative techniques, and that the profiling methods may be helpful in some investigations. But the judges also ruled that linkage analysis was not reliable enough to be used as part of a capital murder case. In this particular case, for example, there were many nonlinkage variables: the women were in different states; one was a law enforcement officer in uniform, the other was a single mother leaving a convenience store. There were differences in age, race, weight, and height of the victims. Fortin may have committed both crimes, but simply saying, "They look the same to me, Judge" wasn't admissible evidence.

The Steven Fortin case is just one in the broader picture in which the profiling methodology, in order to be seen as both accurate and reliable, should have been based on empirical research. It must be reproducible. It must not be subject to the whims and hunches of any single individual. It's not that all profiling advice is poor, but rather that many profilers fall in the trap of *cognitive tunnels and cognitive illusions.*

Just as an optical illusion plays a trick on our eyes, so cognitive illusions plays tricks on our minds. Cognitive illusions involve the illusion of "knowing." As the author Massimo Piattelli-Palmarini writes in his book *Inevitable Illusions: How Mistakes of Reason Rule Our Minds*, "These are errors we commit without knowing that we do so, in good faith, and errors that we often defend with vehemence, thus making our power of reasoning subservient to our illusions." Cognitive tunnels are heuristics that operate at the level of consciousness and reasoning. Heuristics are rules of thumb that people use to make estimates of probabilities. Cognitive tunnels are like optical illusions in two respects—they lead us to wrong conclusions from information, and their apparent correctness persists even when we have been shown the trick.

What impact do cognitive illusions have on criminal profilers and the decisions they make? Investigators and profilers alike make decisions based on their belief in the validity of the cognitive illusions that they experience, regardless of whether their beliefs are right or wrong. What makes these illusions so dangerous is that people believe in them so much that they would lay money down on their validity.

Until profilers bring science into the picture, until profilers stop relying on horoscope banalities or seductive tales of murder, until profilers start relying on hard research and thousands of critical data points to analyze cases—until then, there will never be an antidote to the poison that is killing the field of profiling.

CHAPTER **6**

THE SNIPER (2002)

AFTER 9/11, IT SEEMED like the nation needed a respite. Instead, a little over one year later, the Sniper took his rifle into the shadows of Washington, D.C., Virginia, and Maryland, and the nation held its collective breath.

In the fall of 2002, the Sniper first struck in the D.C. area. On Wednesday, October 2, at 6:04 P.M. when a shot came out of the gathering dusk and killed James D. Martin, fifty-five, of Silver Spring, Maryland, in a grocery store parking lot in Wheaton, Maryland. Just getting started, the Sniper drove out for the next round of violence.

On Thursday, October 3, at 7:41 A.M., James L. "Sonny" Buchanan, thirty-nine, of Arlington, Virginia, was shot and killed while cutting grass at an auto dealership in the White Flint, Maryland, area. At 8:12 A.M., Prem Kumar Walekar, fifty-four, a taxi driver from Olney, Maryland, was shot and killed as he pumped gas at a station in the Aspen Hill, Maryland, area. Just twenty-five minutes later, at 8:37 A.M., the Sniper shot Sarah Ramos, thirty-four, outside of a post office in Silver Spring. At 9:58 A.M., Lori Ann Lewis-Rivera, twenty-five, of Silver Spring was shot and killed while she vacuumed her van at a gas station in Kensington, Maryland.

Ballistics linked the shootings to one gun. The police were in a panic. Whoever the Sniper was, he slipped in and out of areas undetected. Clearly not a serial killer, because there was no cooling off period between kills, the Sniper appeared to be a spree killer, killing people sporadically but close together in time. This was confirmed when, for the fourth time that day, the Sniper struck. At 9:15 P.M., Pascal Charlot, seventy-two, was shot and killed while standing on a street in Washington.

Montgomery County police chief Charles Moose, whose department spearheaded the sniper task force, seemed to be totally ineffectual. The killings continued. On Friday October 4 at 2:30 A.M., a forty-three-year-old Spotsylvania, Virginia, woman got lucky. Shot in the back in a parking lot at a craft store in Fredericksburg, Virginia, she would be hospitalized and released on Tuesday, October 8. Meanwhile, on October 7, a thirteen-year-old student in Bowie, Maryland, was shot in the chest outside his school at 8:08 A.M. He was lucky, too, and survived the attack, but only after undergoing a three-hour operation to remove the bullet.

By that time, the Sniper, the name having stuck from the first media reports, smelled blood, and struck yet again. On the evening of Wednesday, October 9, at 8:18 P.M., Dean Harold Meyers, fifty-three, of Gaithersburg, Maryland, was shot to death just after pumping and paying for fuel at a Manassas, Virginia, Sunoco station.

The Sniper came back on the morning of Friday, October 11, to do some more business. At 9:30 A.M. Kenneth H. Bridges of Philadelphia, age fifty-three, was gunned down while pumping gas at a Massaponax, Virginia, Exxon station on Route 1, just south of

Fredricksburg. The next victim was FBI agent Linda Franklin, forty-seven, of Arlington, Virginia. At 9:15 on Monday evening, October 14, she was shot in the head as she and her husband loaded packages into their car in a crowded Home Depot parking lot in Falls Church, Virginia. It would be another five days before the Sniper struck again on Saturday, October 19, at 8:00 P.M. A thirty-seven-year-old man was shot in the abdomen as he and his wife walked to their car outside a Ponderosa restaurant in Ashland, Virginia. A resident of Melbourne, Florida, he would undergo two operations for extensive damage to multiple organs and survive.

As the nation held its breath waiting for the police to track down the murderer, the Sniper continued, on Tuesday morning, October 22, at 5:56 A.M.. Conrad Johnson, thirty-five, a commuter bus driver, was struck by a single bullet as he was preparing for his morning bus route in Aspen Hill, Maryland. He later died of his injuries. All the networks broadcast dramatic dawn footage of the crime scene.

Robert Holmes, forty-seven, from Tacoma, Washington, and Whitney Donahue, thirty eight, from Greencastle, Pennsylvania, were finally credited with providing the tips that lead to the apprehension of the John Allen Muhammad and Lee Boyd Malvo.

Holmes had met John Muhammad when the two enlisted in the Army in 1985. Holmes testified at Muhammad's trial in 2003 that he called the FBI on October 15, 2002. He had become suspicious after seeing a television report about the October 14 shooting of FBI analyst Linda Franklin in the Home Depot parking lot in Falls Church, Virginia.

Whitney Donahue spotted the Chevrolet Caprice being used by Muhammad and Malvo, at a Maryland rest area on October 24. He called police and remained on the phone with dispatchers for hours until police surrounded the car and arrested both suspects.

John Allan Muhammad had qualified as an expert marksman in the service. His ward, seventeen-year-old John Lee Malvo, a Jamaican citizen, would later admit to killing several of the victims. The nation was relieved that the spree was over but surprised that the Sniper was two. I wasn't.

The devastation spree killings bring to families is incalculable, especially when perpetrated by men like Muhammad and Malvo whose kill total hits the teens. Murder ripples through generations like some primordial seismic wave. Every friend, every relative of the people these men killed will be irreversibly affected by the deaths of their loved ones. In generations to come, those effects will be palpably felt.

Doctorate in hand, I flew back to America. My intent was to support myself as a university professor by day. By night I would become a modern-day tracker, and my prey would be serial killers. Instead, I ran head-on into a brick wall.

Just like anything else, there was competition for jobs. I may have been the only formally trained psycho-geographic profiler operating in America, but that and two bucks got me on the New York subway. What sold was the straight FBI line. The only job I could find was as an adjunct professor and grant writer at the University of Alaska, Anchorage.

A southerner in Alaska doesn't quite work. After two years, I was lucky enough to get a job as an assistant professor of justice studies at Methodist College in my home state of North Carolina. Very quietly, I began to consult with police departments and media outlets on serial murder cases. When the Sniper struck in October 2002, CNN asked me to appear as an on-air expert with a psycho-geographic profile of the sniper.

I repeatedly stated the following on national TV, radio, and newspaper interviews:

1. IT WAS NOT ONE SNIPER BUT TWO.
2. THE KILLERS HAD A TIM MCVEIGH-TYPE MENTALITY, A PARA-MILITARY ATTITUDE. THIS CLEARLY APPLIES TO MUHAMMAD.
3. THERE WAS A VIRGINIA CONNECTION TO THESE KILLINGS. I MAIN-TAINED THAT THE HOME BASE WOULD BE IN THE NORTHERN VIRGINIA AREA, DOWN TOWARD THE POINT OF THE WEDGE. MUHAMMAD'S LAST KNOWN ADDRESS IN THE REGION WAS IN CLINTON, MARYLAND (HIS SECOND EX-WIFE'S HOME), WHICH IS LOCATED IN THE WEDGE NOT FAR FROM ONE OF MY PREDICTED TARGET AREAS, WALDORF, MARYLAND. I ACTUALLY PREDICTED THAT THE MAIN ANCHOR POINT WAS SLIGHTLY NORTH OF DALE CITY, VIRGINIA, WHICH IS NEAR CLINTON, MARYLAND.

I-95 SNIPER GEOGRAPHICAL PROFILE

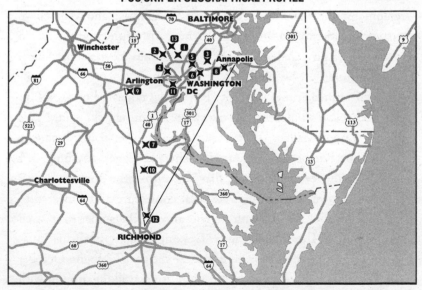

Lines indicate wedge theory   Numbers indicate sequence of shootings

Next, I brought Predator into action. I came on the sniper scene October 3, after Sarah Ramos was killed in Silver Spring, Maryland, while sitting on a beach in front of a restaurant. Four had been killed by that time.

I was the first and only individual to predict that the sniper would move south along I-95, which I first stated on October 5 on several local and national radio shows and then on CNN October 8. During that CNN interview, I predicted, based on my analysis of serial killers, that Fredericksburg, Virginia, would likely be the next target area—which it was, three days later. In regard to the shooting in Falls Church, Virginia, you will notice that this location is located directly in the middle of the wedge.

Would Muhammad and Malvo have been caught if law enforcement had staked out Fredericksburg with cops on October 11? Or would the snipers have just looked for another venue to continue their terror reign? At worst, if the police had used my geographic profile, they would have made Muhammad and Malvo have to work harder to kill. Instead of science, authorities and the media preferred to give credence to the FBI/Thomas Harris serial killer/profiler model.

Self-trained criminal profiler Pat Brown appeared on CNN on October 11. Commenting on the sniper shootings, she said, "This guy is a psychopath. . . . He's involved in power control, and he might like Rambo movies, Arnold Schwarzenegger, anything that gives him the feeling of power, that he controls the universe."

Ms. Brown's comments were total conjecture and appeared to be pulled out of thin air with no relevance to the sniper case. Even the retired FBI profiler Candice DeLong bought into this junk. According to a transcript of an interview she gave CNN on October 16: "I see him all into this stealth ninja stuff, walking around with a swagger, used to bossing people around, maybe a fireman or construction worker." Delong swore that the sniper was under twenty-five and worked alone. However, it turned out that John Muhammad was forty-one when arrested and had a partner, Lee Malvo, who was seventeen.

Another profiler, Brent Turvey, told the *Washington Times* that "the [sniper] was so exact in the attacks that he was unlikely to contact police or give away any evidence that would help investigators."

Turvey was wrong. The break in the sniper case came when a call from Lee Malvo mentioned a fatal liquor-store shooting in Montgomery, Alabama. Evidence from that crime led to a home in Tacoma, Washington, and then to the suspects' blue Chevy in Maryland.

The person whom some would consider the father of criminal profiling, retired FBI profiler Robert Ressler, weighed in on the sniper media hype. "What happened with the sniper case was not really profiling; the networks brought on a cast of clowns," Ressler told the *Daily Iowan* newspaper.

Ressler seemed to contradict himself when he made a statement regarding the personality of the sniper who had left a Tarot card at the scene of one of the shootings. The sniper, Ressler said, could be "into weird mysticism . . . and possibly [the role-playing game] Dungeons & Dragons. He's fascinated with the unusual." Ressler also predicted, confidently, that the killer would be white.

Tarot is practiced by millions of people worldwide. To go from that to "weird mysticism" and Dungeons & Dragons requires a gigantic leap of deductive logic. Using the same logic, one could suggest that because the killer used a car to make a getaway, he was an accomplished mechanic, and a fanatical fan of *Starsky and Hutch*. Ressler was wrong on all counts. The killers were not mystics, fortune-tellers, role players, or white.

Then there was former New York City homicide detective Bo Dietl. A frequent guest of radio's Don Imus, Dietl guessed that "two skinny kids" were doing the shooting and claimed victory when the police apprehended two men. Among some so-called experts, there was even confusion whether the sniper shootings were the work of a serial killer. Jack Levin, a well-known criminologist, stated on *The Larry King Show* on October 18, 2002: "You know, Larry, we're talking about a serial killer because he kills one victim at a time over a long period." Mr. Levin misstated the definition of serial murder. Serial killings have a longer time frame than just two weeks, many lasting months and even years. The D.C.-area shootings took place in a two-week time span, which at that time made the shootings a *spree*.

Despite his obvious proficiency with a rifle, the weapon that killed all the victims, even military experts had insisted the sniper was not a soldier. A soldier would have chosen the more accurate .308 caliber bullet that the military issues, not the .223 used by the sniper, the experts said. However, John Muhammad was an eleven-year Army veteran who fought during the Gulf War. When confronted by this anomaly, the police maintained that the .223 caliber bullet was his signature.

The claims of these profilers were little more than anecdotal accounts, on par with the claims of psychics and astrologers. It is also important to point out that their profiling claims were wrong, dead wrong. Even when confronted with facts to the contrary, some profilers don't accept responsibility for wrong opinions.

It is often difficult to see how most profilers have reached their conclusions. For example, Gregg McCrary, former FBI profiler and instructor at the FBI Academy's profiling unit, made this statement to the *Washington Post* about the I-95 sniper: "When you break down the demographics of the Washington region, there is a statistical probability that the sniper is a white man."

The United States has always stood, and always will, as a shining beacon of liberty and opportunity to those who for one reason or another didn't get a fair shake in their country of origin. In recent years, many immigrants coming to the United States have been from the Caribbean, some of them illegally.

The second part of the sniper team was Lee Boyd Malvo, seventeen at the time of the killings. He was born in the slums of Kingston, Jamaica, in February 1985 to Leslie Malvo, a bricklayer, and Una James, a scamstress. Malvo's parents never married and separated when he was just a few years old. After the separation, Malvo lived with his mother and rarely saw his father.

As a child, Malvo's mother traveled to find work. When she did, Malvo was left with relatives and friends, sometimes for long periods of time. Dissatisfied with such a life, James left Jamaica when Malvo was about fourteen months old and moved with him to Antigua, hoping to find a better life there for her son. People in Antigua who remember Malvo later described him as a friendly teenager, respectful to the person they thought was his father but was really Muhammad.

While living in Antigua in 2000, Malvo and his mother had met Gulf War vet and U.S. citizen John Allen Muhammad. James would later deny any sort of intimate relationship with Muhammad while admitting that her son and Muhammad had eventually formed a strong bond. James told a Jamaican TV interviewer that her son had spent most of his life seeking a father figure.

She neglected to mention that the man he chose, John Allan

Muhammad, was a classic con man. In May, 2001, Muhammad arranged for Malvo and James to be part of an illegal immigration ploy involving a cargo ship traveling from Jamaica to Florida. Muhammad had his ward Malvo traveling under the passport of his actual son, Limburg Williams, who had never set foot on Antigua.

When the ship got to Miami, many of the illegals, including Malvo and James, jumped ship rather than face customs. James would later admit to U.S. Customs agents that she and her son were passengers on a cargo ship that was filled with "illegal Asians [sic]." They were all off-loaded in the Miami area where she immediately found work at the Red Lobster in Fort Myers, Florida.

Muhammad longed to visit his first wife in Washington State. He convinced James and Malvo to come with him. Malvo was finally caught by the border patrol in Bellingham, Washington, in December 2001. What had happened was that the local cops had called the border patrol during an incident involving "some sort of custody dispute" between two individuals later identified as Una James and Muhammad. All three were traveling together.

The authorities knew nothing of Muhammad's supplying Malvo with a false name. Muhammad was a U.S. citizen, free to go. INS records indicate that neither mother nor son had any documents proving their identities or allowing them entry to the United States. Clearly, they were illegal aliens. The border patrol agents decided that because James had "no roots or close family ties in the United States" she was likely to abscond.

The arresting officer wrote that the mother-and-son illegal aliens, Lee Boyd Malvo and Una James, would be "detained at the Seattle Detention facility in Seattle, Washington pending deportation charges." In direct violation of federal law, Malvo and James were freed by the INS district in Seattle. It would later be looked at as just another snafu in a system full of them.

Teaming up with Muhammad, Malvo left Washington in the summer of 2002 and traveled to Baton Rouge, Louisiana. For Muhammad, Baton Rouge was no accident; another of Muhammad's ex-wives lived there. That ex-wife thing would prove to be Muhammad's ultimate undoing.

After their southern sojourn, Muhammad and Malvo headed north. Muhammad went to the Washington, D.C., area with a clear motive in mind: to seek out, terrorize, and eventually murder his second ex-wife, Mildred Muhammad, who had moved there from Washington State with their three children. According to Mildred's brother Charles Green, Mildred's taking his kids away angered Muhammad more than anything in the world. Muhammad was attached to his children. When he couldn't see the kids anymore, he planned to kill his ex-wife. All the other killings were meant to divert investigators away from Mildred's murder.

Muhammad and Malvo carried a geographical template in their minds that formed a wedge-shaped pattern similar to a piece of pie. They had a certain kind of place in mind where experience had taught them suitable victims could be found. Subsequent trips to these crime locations formed something of an analogy with previous successes, modified by experience and perhaps intelligence gained from previous murders.

In my opinion, John Muhammad's narrative mental map was shaped by stalking his ex-wife, Mildred Muhammad, whose apartment is located in Clinton, Maryland. This is why that I repeatedly stated on major news shows that there was a northern Virginia connection to these shootings—a connection away from the suburbs of Washington, D.C.; Clinton is located near the Virginia state line.

John Muhammad constantly staked out his ex-wife's home— behavior similar to that of a burglar. Decades of research on burglars indicate that most spend hours driving around different communities during the day, predetermining ideal targets and times for their criminal activities.

Of course, all this is an attempt to explain the unexplainable. Of course, no one really knows what goes on inside someone else's brain. But as to Muhammad and Malvo's hearts, there can be no doubt that they are at the very least disturbed.

After they were caught, Virginia and Maryland fought over who would prosecute them first. It was like a lottery, with the lucky state being drawn by Attorney General John Ashcroft. Ashcroft went with Virginia because Virginia not only has the death penalty, it uses it. Maryland also has the death penalty but doesn't use it.

Psychiatrists working for the court were asked to examine documents and drawings taken from Malvo's Fairfax County jail cell. What they found were two drawings he had done of himself, a sniper's scope drawn around his head. His writings focused on the pseudo-mystical pronouncements of the characters in the 1999 Wachowski brothers film *The Matrix*. He wrote of his Muslim faith, lyrics from Bob Marley songs, and musings about the political theories of Thomas Hobbes, John Locke, and Socrates.

The *Washington Post* reported that the shrinks thought the writings could have been the obsessive ruminations of a mentally ill prisoner, or simply the aggressive imagery of an angry teenager. They did agree that, in part, they showed a very confused adolescent who was smart and well read. Like Muhammad, he, too, would eventually be convicted of capital murder. Despite the state's best efforts to put him in the electric chair, Malvo's jury found that his life had value and sentenced him to life in prison without parole.

In this post 9/11 age where individual rights have become an issue in the battle against terrorism, it has become equally obvious that federal law enforcement agencies regularly fail to share intelligence. The FBI has been cited in *The 9/11 Commission Report* as having egregious shortcomings in this regard.

That criticism should extend to the way the Bureau profiles and consequently convinces local police of the efficacy and accuracy of their "data." In the sniper case, the FBI's hollow science, along with Rossmo's wrong profile, misled local investigators. And what about the U.S. Border Patrol in Washington State? Why did they let Malvo and James go, when federal law dictated they be retained. Clearly if Malvo had been deported, he could not have participated with Muhammad in the spree killings of October 2002. These are questions to be pondered, and while we do, lives are being lost.

CHAPTER 7

THE MARDi GRAS EFFECT

AMERICAN PSYCHOLOGISTS REFER TO the ability to hide one's identity on the Internet as the Mardi Gras phenomenon. Internet users feel they are wearing masks and can act anonymously.

In the dark and secretive world of cyberspace, there are individuals seeking to experience weird adventures. Hidden in the cloak of their aliases, some offer to sell their used underwear while others are looking for potential victims to murder. The stage for the fulfillment of these fantasies is an imaginary world created by the visitors to chat rooms and newsgroups on the Internet.

Newsgroups are unmediated areas that provide forums for every topic imaginable. A series of messages, called a thread, is posted for anyone to see and respond to. No one needs to use their real name if they don't want to, and most don't. Instead, participants choose one or more *handles* by which they are known. This handle is their mask.

Chat rooms operate in real time with messages posted and responded to instantly for all participants to see. Private chat rooms can also be arranged. Handles are used here also. This anonymity allows chat room and newsgroup visitors to take on the persona of whomever they wish. It provides the perfect venue for deceit.

Outsiders may question whether individuals are able to maintain their touch with reality when they continuously pretend to be someone that they are not. This might be true for some; for others, this also means exploring their fantasies in ways never before possible. Thirty-five-year-old Sharon Denburg Lopatka from Maryland was someone who trolled around the Internet, little knowing someone was trolling for her, someone else who had bought into the Mardi Gras effect knowingly, and with the worst intent.

Sharon Lopatka boarded the 9:15 passenger train on the morning of October 13, 1996, in her hometown of Hampstead, Maryland. She told her construction worker husband, Victor Lopatka, she was going to visit friends in Georgia, but her ticket said "Charlotte, North Carolina."

In the chat room she frequented, she read the fantasy messages others posted and related her own intimate sexual fantasies. By the standards and norms of the bondage/sadomasochism chat rooms Lopatka frequented, she could feel normal. While the term *BDSM*—bondage, domination, and sadomasochism—is frequently used to describe the type of sex act where one person plays the role of a dominant partner and another takes the submissive role, in general terms it describes the activities of individuals involved in dominant/submissive sexual relations.

While posted messages may be anonymous, they are not private. Among the rules of the BDSM aficionados is the promotion of safety. The only thing Lopatka had in mind was satiation, not safety. She talked of things like strangulation to obtain an orgasm, and insertion of foreign objects into her body. Some tried to prevent her from traveling down this dangerous path. One woman attempted to counsel her over the Internet, but Lopatka rejected her with the response, "I want the real thing. I did not ask for you preaching to me."

Sharon Lopatka was a happily married woman, living in a suburb of Baltimore. Her father, Abraham J. Denburg, was the longtime cantor for the Beth Tfiloh Congregation. When twenty-nine-year-old Sharon, the oldest of four daughters, married Victor Lopatka, a Catholic from Ellicott City, Maryland, in 1991, she considered the marriage an act of rebellion against her parents' Jewish heritage; they considered it sacrilege. Orthodox Jews believe in a literal interpretation of the Old Testament, including a ban against intermarriage with those outside the faith. In some Orthodox Jewish families, when such a marriage happens, the parents of the offending child sit Shiva, the seven-day Jewish mourning period for the dead. Again flouting Orthodox Jewish tradition, she and husband Victor did not have children.

All Lopatka's friends thought her to be a normal, well-adjusted middle-class housewife, but you never know what happens when the door closes at night. Behind the facade, Sharon was miserable, unhappy, and sexually frustrated. She and Vic spent little time together. She did not work outside her home, and when she discovered the Internet, she had the time and the opportunity to explore it completely. Sharon discovered the anonymous world of sexual chat rooms, where she poured out her heart and her fantasies to strangers, because they were there and willing to take the time to listen.

Sharon may have been innocent on the Net but she wasn't in her business. On two different Web sites, Lopatka touted psychic services. Her inspiration was a thirty-nine-dollar money-making kit advertised by an Arizona company. It outlined ways she could make money from running Internet advertisements and leasing 900-numbers.

As Craftsy@GNN.com, Sharon posted messages all over the net offering a "FREE Newsletter" on how to turn crafts into money. Under the business name of "Classified Concepts Unlimited," she offered to write or rewrite classified ads, promising "phenomenal results" for her fifty-dollar fee.

"Sit back and then literally watch the orders pour in," she told her unsuspecting audience. On two other Web pages, "Psychics Know All" and "Dionne Enterprises," she promoted psychic hot lines. By day she made money from her phony businesses. By night, she let the Mardi Gras phenomenon overtake her, becoming the well-built femme fatale "Nancy," or the 250 pound dominatrix "Gina." On August 2, 1996, she wrote in one chat room:

"DO YOU DARE ENTER . . . THE LAND OF THE GIANTESS??? Where men are crushed like bugs . . . by these angry . . . yet gorgeous giant goddesses."

Fantasies, Sharon had them all. She was everything from a porno actress to necrophilia aficionado.

"Hi, my name is Gina. . . . I kind of have a fascination with torturing till death . . . of course I can't speak about it with my friends or family. Would love to have an e-mail exchange with someone."

When her Internet lovers realized she was serious, that she wanted a real time (r/t) encounter to enact her death fantasies, her "loves" stopping writing her. Except for one. One man continued his communication with Sharon. His name was Robert Glass. His net handle was "Slowhand." Between August and October 1996, they exchanged over nine hundred e-mails. Over half contained graphic sadomasochistic fantasies. Unfortunately, Sharon had not chosen well.

Robert "Bobby" Glass was born in rural Caldwell County, North Carolina, on Valentine's Day 1951, and was raised near Lenoir, North Carolina, a small city of about 14,200 that calls itself the "Gateway to the Blue Ridge Mountains." Coming from a good family, with deep roots in the community, Glass was well respected.

Like many in North Carolina's rural areas, Glass lived in a trailer, something he terribly resented; just down the road was the mansion in which he had grown up. His father, Joe Glass, had been a beloved civic figure. Somehow, Robert Glass's life didn't work out the way it was supposed to and he wound up in that trailer. Still, he seemed happily married to his wife, Sherri, with whom he had three kids, ages six, seven, and ten. He belonged to the local Rotary Club, like his father, and had held the same job for sixteen years as a computer analyst for neighboring Catawba County.

During their marriage, Glass encouraged his wife, Sherri, to take a computer class at the local community college. He thought it would build up her self-confidence. Sherri later stated, "He knew his computers. They were his passion, too. Computers became his life. He ate, slept everything about computers. He would stay up almost all night on the Internet. I'd have to drag him out of bed in the morning to go to work." They separated in early 1996.

Glass used an IBM-compatible PC with a slow 66 megahertz (clock speed) and only 8 megabytes of RAM. Antiquated by current standards, it was considered a moderately powerful computer in 1996. A subscriber of America Online (AOL), in his online profile Slowhand said he loved photography, music, and model railroads. Under personal quotes, he wrote, "Moderation in all things, including moderation." It was actually a paraphrase of what the High Lama says to the hero in James Hilton's *Lost Horizon*. It was also a lie. He was into BDSM.

Lopatka and Glass met in an online chat room. They exchanged S&M fantasies and agreed to finally meet after months of e-mail and chat room correspondence. This was how Sharon Lopatka, the daughter of Orthodox Jews, happily married to Vic, came to take her ill-fated trip to Charlotte, North Carolina. Like in some hammy country western song, her dream man Glass met her at the station. He took her to his ramshackle trailer in the backcountry of Colletsville.

Trailer trash was exactly what Glass had all over the interior of his 10' x 50' turquoise blue house trailer, which sat on a desolate lawn littered with rusting toys and rotten produce. In the dank trailer, dirty dishes were mixed in with computer disks and computer magazines. Whatever the place was, it didn't deter Lopatka, who decided to stay. For three days, the happy couple acted the fantasies they had only previously talked about. They were violent and lurid, the stuff tabloids feed on.

Glass would tie a rope around Lopatka's neck during sex, cutting off oxygen to her brain. This enabled her to experience a strange euphoria as she climaxed. Some who practice this, called autoerotic asphyxiation, actually die from it. Other times, Lopatka's hands and feet were bound by rope to Glass' bed while he probed her vagina and anus with foreign objects. It was during one of these sadomasochistic acts that Sharon Lopatka stopped breathing and died.

Lopatka's large body was a burden for the short, paunchy, and middle-aged Glass to move. Realizing he would never be able to carry her to his car, he moved with alacrity. A short way off his lawn, Glass dug a grave on the path he used from his house to a backyard trash pit. It was the best he could do. He dragged Sharon down to the makeshift grave and buried her. He covered her up as best he could and went back to his usual life as a computer analyst for Catawba County like nothing had happened.

On October 20, Vic Lopatka discovered a note that his wife had left. It stated, "If my body is never retrieved, don't worry; know that I am at peace." Immediately, he filed a missing person report with his local police department. Maryland police investigated and found no indication of anyone in Sharon Lopatka's background who would want to do her harm. She was well liked and respected by everyone.

The Maryland detectives decided to check out Lopatka's computer for a clue to her disappearance. That's when they found hundreds of sexually oriented messages about torture and murder that had been exchanged with a male who used the computer handle Slowhand. Specifically, Slowhand had written that he was going to sexually torture Lopatka and then kill her.

On the application for a search warrant, investigators said the messages "described in detail how Slowhand was going to sexually torture the missing person and ultimately kill her." The investigators backtracked the trail through Internet and state lines, through online S&M and bondage chat rooms and newsgroups, until they discovered the true identity of Slowhand to be Robert Glass.

Without hard evidence, like a confession or the discovery of a body, the Maryland police didn't fully believe that Lopatka would board that train for a date with her murderer. On October 22, they began surveillance on Glass, hoping he would lead them to Lopatka, whom they doggedly believed was alive.

Glass's routine was uneventful; Lopatka never appeared. On October 25, police obtained a search warrant. While Glass was at work, they searched his home. From the trailer, police removed boxes filled with thousands of computer disks; bondage and drug paraphernalia; a pistol; videotapes; Glass's computer; and, what appeared to be items of Lopatka's that matched the description her husband had given the police.

One of the investigators searching the trailer's grounds noticed newly turned dirt a short distance down the path from the trailer's front door. They only had to dig down a few feet down before they found Lopatka. Her hands and feet were still bound with rope, and she had a piece of nylon cord around her neck. Detectives also found scrapes on her breasts and neckline.

The day after Robert Glass's arrest, October 26, 1996, North Carolina superior court Judge Beverly T. Beal placed a gag order on investigators and attorneys. They were not to talk to the media. Glass was indicted for first degree murder and ordered held without bond. It would take the authorities three years to categorize a mountain of case evidence. While the delay was a bit unusual, it is not uncommon. Police regularly arrest suspects without enough evidence to convict them for the crimes they're charged with. An indictment is merely that, but it's enough to put a defendant behind bars while the system goes to work to convict the defendant. In the Lopatka case, the system worked.

After the three-year investigation, there was certainly enough to get a conviction on second degree, willful murder charges if the jury saw the things the prosecution's way. If they didn't, there could be an acquittal. Anyone who has ever had anything to do with the criminal justice system knows that you never know what a jury will do. As for the defense, they had a tough road to hoe. During the discovery phase prior to trial, both sides exchange evidence and witness lists. From the evidence the prosecution was ready to bring to trial, it became evident there was a good chance of conviction. On January 27, 1999, Glass took a plea.

Robert Glass pleaded guilty to involuntary manslaughter. Glass also pleaded guilty to six counts of second-degree sexual exploitation of a minor, a charge that developed after police discovered child pornography on his computer. As part of his plea, the prosecution demanded that Glass describe how Lopatka died and what his contribution was.

Glass explained to the court how Lopatka had looped a nylon

cord around her neck. He couldn't recall how much he had pulled on the rope. All he could say for certain was that he never wanted to kill her, but one way or another she ended up dead anyway.

While Lopatka's family had signed off on the plea agreement—it is standard practice in a homicide case for the prosecution to get the family of the victim to agree to the deal before it is accepted—a statement by Lopatka's relatives said that Glass "took advantage of [Lopatka's] situation. He could have walked away. He debased not only her but her body after she was dead."

Caldwell County superior court judge Claude Sitton sentenced Glass to thirty-six to fifty-three months for manslaughter and twenty-one to twenty-six months for the first of the six other charges. Sentences for the other five counts were suspended. He also got federal time, twenty-seven months, on the child pornography charges, three years supervised release, and participation in a sex offender program for possessing child pornography.

Robert Glass wound up at the Avery-Mitchell Correctional Institution in the North Carolina mountains. With time off for good behavior, he was given parole on March 6, 2002, but didn't make the date. On February 20, 2002, Glass had a massive coronary and died before he could be released.

Luckily, Glass only murdered once. There are some sadistic individuals that rely on the Mardi Gras Effect to lure and murder repeatedly. For several women, their online bondage and sadomasochistic fantasies led to their real-time deaths at the hands of serial killer John Robinson, aka the "Slavemaster" of Kansas and Missouri.

CHAPTER **8**

THE SLAVE MASTER

JOHN EDWARD ROBINSON WAS the third of five children, born in the Chicago suburb of Cicero on December 27, 1943. He was a Boy Scout, achieving the Scouts' highest award, Eagle Scout, by fourteen. So popular was Robinson that he was chosen as the sole American representative to lead 120 boy scouts at the Royal Command Performance in London in front of Queen Elizabeth II.

By age twenty-one, Robinson seemed to be on the fast track; he was married to Nancy Lynch and working in the back office of a hospital. It wasn't long, however, before he had to leave Chicago after being accused of embezzling money from his employer. He later moved west to Kansas City, Kansas.

Soon after arriving in Kansas City in 1965, Robinson got a job as an X-ray technician at Children's Mercy Hospital. He was later fired from that position for incompetence. In 1966, he managed to charm his way into actually running the lab at Fountain Plaza X-Ray Laboratory. Robinson was later fired for embezzling $33,000 from the business, although it's thought that he had stolen more like $200,000. Found guilty of embezzling only the $33,000, he lucked out and received a suspended sentence and three years' probation.

But Robinson just didn't get the message. He was arrested again in 1971 for stealing, once again from his employers.

By that time, he had moved around a lot. Tired of working for others, Robinson set up his own business, Professional Services Association, Inc., which was supposed to provide financial consulting to doctors in the Kansas City area. It was nothing but a shadow business for his latest crime: forgery. In 1975, Robinson was caught forging signatures and letters in an attempt to claim thousands of dollars via a stock scam. The U.S. Securities and Exchange Commission investigated and charged Robinson's company with securities fraud, mail fraud, and false representation. Robinson pleaded it out and was fined $2,500 and placed on three years' probation. And, of course, he continued his criminal career.

In 1977, Robinson invented a new award, Kansas City "Man of the Year," and not only claimed it in its first year but tricked state senator Mary Gant into presenting him with the plaque. The *Kansas City Star* ran a story about the award. The paper received numerous protests that the award wasn't fair. A reporter was sent to investigate the claim. The *Star* ran a follow-up story, exposing Robinson's criminal history and his convictions on fraud charges. He faded into the background.

In June 1981, Robinson was charged with the felony theft from a former employer, Guy's Foods in Liberty, where he had served as employee relations manager. Again, Robinson dealt, pleading guilty to stealing a check worth $6,000, and was ordered to pay back $50,000 to Guy's Foods. Amazingly, he used his charm to eke out a sixty-day jail sentence and five years' probation. He was released in July 1982. Soon afterward, Robinson's scams started to turn decidedly weird. He started up a prostitution service out of a shabby apartment he rented in Kansas City. He kept several mistresses at once, often putting them up in low-rent KC apartments. Some of them he sexually abused.

In 1984, a stout, well-dressed, middle-aged man who identified himself as John Osborne walked into the Truman Medical Center in Independence, Missouri. He told Karen Gaddis, a social worker in the hospital's ob-gyn unit, that he was a founder of a program to help out homeless mothers. Gaddis was suspicious and later recalled thinking, "We were a fertile ground for what he was *really* looking for: young women nobody could trace." John Osborne was actually John Robinson, and Gaddis was absolutely right.

Robinson found his first victim in Lisa Stasi, a pretty, curly-haired nineteen-year-old Alabaman with a four-month-old daughter. She and her unemployed husband, Carl, had split, leaving her with the responsibilities of a single mother. On New Year's Eve 1984, she checked into a battered-women's shelter in Independence, Missouri. Feeling depressed and vulnerable, Stasi was more than willing to accept John Robinson's offer to help, this time calling himself Frank Osborne. He promised to get her a job and a place to stay. Stasi figured she'd finally caught a break.

Robinson rented Room 131 for Stasi and her daughter Tiffany at the Rodeway Inn, in the Kansas City suburb of Overland Park. Stasi noticed that there were other women at the Rodeway Inn who seemed to know Frank Osborn. Robinson told Stasi they were other outreach moms, but Stasi thought that they looked just like prostitutes.

Stasi had been missing for a few weeks. Letters sent from the shelter to family members carried Stasi's signature and explained that she was fine and her baby was healthy, but the letters were type-written, and Stasi could not type. Her sister-in-law, Kathy Klingin-smith, went to the police station in Overland Park to file a missing-persons report on Stasi and her daughter. Almost immedi-ately the Overland Park detectives began to suspect John Robinson; he had paid for the room that Stasi stayed in with his American Express card in the business name of Equi-II.

Investigators discovered that other women close to Robinson had suddenly gone missing. Among them was nineteen-year-old Paula Godfrey, an auburn-haired former figure skater who had gone to work as a sales rep for Equi-II. She vanished in 1984. Another missing woman was Korean-born Catherine Clampitt, twenty-seven, also an Equi-II employee. She was reported missing in June 1987. But, as with Godfrey and Stasi, no physical evidence of a crime could be found. Due to the lack of forensic evidence, the investigation against John Robinson stalled. Then Robinson got another lucky break.

In 1986 Robinson, then forty-three, was sentenced to serve five and fourteen years for swindling investors in a partnership that organized phony backache seminars. The missing-persons investigations were dropped as Robinson went to prison for fraud. When he was released in 1989, it was into the new world of the Internet. Robinson saw the net as just another avenue for luring victims into his web.

Robinson had his wife Nancy put up a front for him, making believe he was using the computer to make money. He was, but with the same type of illegal scams he had done before, this time with instantaneous results via e-mail. He began to frequent chat rooms and discussion groups that appealed to people's prurient natures. The sadomasochistic/bondage milieu was one he particularly enjoyed, especially people known as "subs," or submissives; they were Robinson's real prey.

Using his handle "Midwest Slavemaster," Robinson trolled the chat rooms and user groups. He became a Net addict, intoxicated by the psychological thrill of the impending kill. Robinson seductively conned lonely, vulnerable women he met in chat rooms. He would then meet them in person, seduce them, and have their mail forwarded to a mailbox that he controlled. After he killed them, he made a substantial income from cashing their government checks, alimony payments, whatever checks were sent to them. Between the mid-nineties and 2000, John Robinson murdered seven women whom he either met online or through newspaper personal ads.

His first known murder victim was Beverly Bonner, a librarian in the Missouri corrections system. Robinson seduced her during his incarceration. Shortly after Robinson got out of a Kansas prison, Bonner made the mistake that would cost her life. She divorced her husband, a prison doctor, and moved to Olathe, Kansas, to work for Robinson in one of his businesses.

Bonner told her ex-husband she was going to be traveling abroad and gave him a post office box address where he should mail her alimony checks. Shortly after the move, Bonner disappeared. Robinson put her belongings in a storage locker in Raymore, Missouri. Included among those "belongings" was a chemical drum. Inside was Beverly Bonner's corpse. Next to the drum were two other barrels.

The next two victims were sisters who came from Fullerton, California. Sheila and Debbie Faith lived a lonely life there. Sheila's husband had died, and Debbie suffered from some sort of neurological disorder that at various times had been diagnosed as spinal bifida or cerebral palsy. Confined to a wheelchair, Debbie had just enough strength to manipulate her wheelchair's joystick controller.

It was after her husband died that Sheila Faith started going online to meet guys; that's how she came to meet John Robinson in an online chat room. Robinson made himself out to be one heckuva wealthy dude. He offered to "keep" her and to pay for her sister Debbie's physiotherapy. Sheila and Debbie quickly packed up their stuff and set of across the country to be with Robinson in Kansas City.

The first thing Robinson had The Faiths do was open a post office box where Debbie's federal disability check could be sent. The second thing Robinson did was kill them. For sometime afterward, the post office box continued to receive Debbie's Social Security Insurance checks and just like clockwork, every month, John Robinson came by and picked them up. As for Sheila and Debbie Faith, Robinson put their bodies in chemical drums in the Raymore storage locker.

Next, Robinson began a relationship with beautiful college student named Izabela Lewicka. A Polish immigrant, she lived in north-central Indiana with her parents, who were university professors. Lewicka was interested in studying fine arts. In late 1997, she suddenly informed her parents that she was dropping out of Purdue University.

Free of her parents' yoke, Lewicka headed for Kansas City. A rich businessman she had met online had offered her an internship. He was a publisher, she told her family, and it was too good an opportunity to pass up. What Lewicka didn't tell her parents was that she had agreed to be Robinson's slave. They would never see or speak to her again.

After she moved to Kansas City, Robinson gave her a ring and took the innocent Lewicka to the county registrar's office. They paid for a marriage license that was never picked up. She told her parents they were married but never told them her husband's name. Strangely, the "couple" didn't live together; in public, Robinson sometimes said he was her uncle. This was a role he could certainly play, however different from the real one: Robinson was now a real life Slave master.

Part of the deal Robinson had with Lewicka was that she was the submissive one in their relationship, his slave. She confirmed that by signing a 115-item slave contract. It actually gave Robinson control over her financial affairs. Eventually, however, Robinson grew tired of the young Polish girl. Before she disappeared, Lewicka told her friends that Robinson was taking her on a long trip. They would be gone for a long time. Unfortunately, it was to be longer than she realized. Lewicka was never seen alive again, and someplace another drum was filled with human remains.

While he was taking care of Lewicka, Robinson was busy finding his new love. He met yet another woman online, Suzette Trouten from Michigan, and convinced her to come to Kansas City, where he said he would take care of her. A licensed practical nurse bored with her life, Trouten led the archetypal double life: nurse by day, submissive slave by night. No one knew that beneath her ordinary clothes, she wore a silver chain that hung from rings pierced through her nipples, and had also pierced even more intimate parts of her anatomy. Frequenting many of the same chat rooms as the cyber-ubiquitous Robinson, the two found each other and Trouten fell in love. Robinson passed himself off as a mysterious well-to-do businessman, in need of a full-time caregiver to look after his elderly father who was close to kicking the bucket. Robinson told Trouten that he would pay her more than $60,000 a year in salary, which would go a long way in Kansas's stagnant economy. Moreover, Robinson said he had plans for them to become world travelers.

The twenty-seven-year-old Trouten was extremely close to her mother, whom she spoke to on the phone constantly. She had a number of e-mail and chat room friends, in many of whom she confided her love for Robinson and her pending move to Kansas to work for a man who called himself "J.R.," after Larry Hagman's viciously lovable character on the TV show *Dallas*.

Before leaving Michigan in February, Trouten wrote an e-mail to a friend: "We all finally find what we want and need and I found mine."

When Trouten's mother reported her missing after not hearing from her for a few weeks, police interviewed Robinson, who had aroused police suspicion earlier. Police believed Robinson responsible for the murders of Trouten, Lewicka, Stasi, Godfrey, and Catherine Clampitt, who was twenty-seven years old when she disappeared in 1987, after moving to Overland Park, Kansas, to take a job with John Robinson.

For his part, Robinson was beginning to have some problems. He was losing control. The frequency of his killings was increasing as his insatiable urges could no longer be quieted. Perhaps it was his overconfidence, psychosis, or an unconscious will to get caught. Whatever it was, Robinson was getting sloppy; he was doing a poor job of covering his tracks, forensically and otherwise. The cops were closing in.

Meanwhile, Suzette Trouten's mother Carolyn received several typed letters purportedly from her daughter. The letters had Kansas City postmarks and were uncharacteristically mistake-free. Suzette Trouten was a poor speller, and she never typed notes to friends or family. Carolyn Trouten called the telephone numbers her daughter had given her. Robinson answered the phone.

This was odd. According to Trouten's letters, she was traveling abroad with Robinson, which he promptly denied. He claimed that she had run off with an acquaintance and stolen money from him. Carolyn Trouten reported her daughter missing to the police, who later got warrants to wiretap Robinson's phone and monitor his online activities. What Carolyn Trouten didn't know at the time was that the cops had zeroed in on Robinson as their prime suspect. Carolyn's complaint only helped that process along by giving them more power to monitor Robinson and his activities.

What the police didn't know at first was that Trouten's online friends had grown troubled by her disappearance. They thought it strange she was not around. That's when Robinson, sensing their suspicion, contacted some of Trouten's friends and relatives by e-mail, pretending to be Trouten. Most weren't taken in, and believed it was someone pretending to be Trouten. Robinson dropped the ruse and instead moved forward, as he always did, setting his sites on a new woman: one of Trouten's online friends named Susan Miles, who lived in western Canada.

Also unbeknown to police, Miles and another Canadian had begun an investigation of the man they believed was named "J.R. Turner," the fellow Trouten said she was going off with. Susan found Robinson online in one of the BDSM rooms, and struck up a friendship. Robinson moved in quickly when Miles told him she was interested in finding a dominant master for a friend.

Soon, their real-timing it with phone calls was picked up by the police wiretaps. The Lenexa, Kansas, police contacted Miles and told her they were investigating John Robinson. They did not explain the nature of the investigation but asked her to continue her relationship with him. Suddenly, the hunter had become the hunted.

"The police didn't tell me to get John Robinson to lure me to Kansas City. I was willing to help," Miles would say later. Robinson made vague offers about meeting in person. "He offered nothing other than I would be financially taken care of and never have to work."

Robinson, of course, had other fish he was trying to catch. Online, he was quick to strike up conversations that became telephone relationships. He was meeting women locally and had struck up an online and telephone friendship with a Texas woman who fit his usual pattern.

Susan Russo was an unemployed psychologist who suffered from depression. She was eager for a change in her life, and

Robinson quickly picked up on this vulnerability. Convincing her he was a powerful community leader who could help her get a start in the Kansas City area, he encouraged her to move to Kansas City. Reluctant to suddenly drop everything and move to Kansas City, she hesitated, telling Robinson she couldn't afford to move. He responded that he'd pay for everything until she had an income of her own.

Tapping the call, the cops knew Susan Russo was the Slave-master's next victim. They watched as, over the Easter/Passover holiday, Robinson wired her money. Russo used the money to travel to Overland Park. Once there, it was time to play. Police listened in on the party.

Robinson, an inconsequential-looking man, was incredibly brutal. He forced Russo to engage in sex acts against her will. He shot photos when Russo was tied up despite her pleas not to. He slapped her with a lot more strength than she expected. He took her money and then turned her out before she was scheduled to return home. He ordered her to return to Texas and await his further instructions. Robinson kept the S&M toys and props she had brought with her.

After returning home, Russo had a chance to reflect on recent events and wrote Robinson an e-mail breaking off their relationship. He didn't like that. He replied:

I just returned and I am one pissed MASTER. You called me when my phone was forwarded to another fucking country and then hung up? What was that all about? Now I get email from you telling me to send your stuf [sic] back and voice mail messages telling me to do the same and that I have taken everything from you. You are correct. I have accepterd [sic] your body, mind and souls [sic], I have accepted you as my slut, whore and slave. I do not do that lightly! You write others to check on me and ask them questions (yes I got

an email from Izzy's MASTER with a copy of your message, he has
punished her severely). If you want out fine, do not contact me again
under any circumstances. I will hold your signed contract, photos
and resume to make sure you do not bother me again . . . as far as
your toys, I will think about it and let you know!!! JR

Russo's response:

To John Edwin Robinson:

It is now 12:00 noon central time as I send you this message.
From this time forward, I do not want to hear from you or your "ref-
erences" by email, letter, and telephone or in person. You will not
respond to this letter, you will abide by it. I will not say or write this
twice. KEEP AWAY FROM ME. IF you do not abide by what I have asked,
I will contact the police and report you for harassing me.

Susan Russo

Once again showing his incredible capacity to move forward like
a shark in the water despite any obstacle, Robinson began stalking a
new victim, Lydia Bustamante, an unemployed dental hygienist.
Meeting her in a BDSM room, he managed to convince her to come
to Overland Park on his dime, which she did. Robinson promised to
give her a job an executive assistant in his hydroponics business.

Taking lodging in the same motel where Russo had stayed
before her abrupt exit, Bustamante waited, alone, for the Slavemaster to return. He let her mind work for a few days before coming
back. He demanded she strip naked and assume a position of his
choosing in a corner of the room. When she refused, Robinson beat
the crap out of her, and then had sex with her.

Bustamante wasn't into extreme physical pain or photography. Robinson couldn't have cared less. He did what he wanted with her and then photographed the bruises on her body. Following his usual pattern, he gave Lydia $100 and sent her home, ordering her to put her possessions in storage and then return to Overland Park. Following his orders, Bustamante did exactly that, but when she returned, Robinson took too much time. He continued to play too rough and left her again, alone, in the motel. This time, Bustamante realized Robinson wasn't the man she'd thought he was.

She called the cops. By that time, a task force had been formed to get the goods on Robinson and take down the Slavemaster. Task force members broke into their motel room and took Bustamante out while Robinson was running an errand. The cops went to Johnson County prosecutor Paul Morrison for an arrest warrant. Eager to get Robinson, Morrison nevertheless needed a more solid and less circumstantial case. Ironically, the help to indict the killer came from the killer himself.

Robinson at the time had also been seducing an Alabama woman who had come close to agreeing to become his slave. Robinson convinced her to come to Kansas City with her eight-year-old daughter. He also made sure to tell her to bring the title to her car. Morrison, of course, would never allow Robinson access to the two, but the phone tap had been enough. That, plus Susan Russo agreeing to file charges against Robinson for stealing her sex toys, meant he could now get an arrest warrant that would stick.

Robinson also murdered Lisa Stasi. Her daughter, Tiffany, was discovered alive in 2001 living in Chicago with Don Robinson, John's brother. Don had assumed that he had legally adopted Tiffany. District Attorney Paul Morrison said during a news conference that John Robinson had been the last person seen with 19-year-old

Lisa Stasi and her four-month-old infant, Tiffany Lynn, before they were reported missing in 1985.

My involvement with the John Robinson case began when Dan Clark, a private investigator, contacted me and expressed an interest in my research on serial killers. Clark referred me to attorney Ron Evans, head of the Kansas Death Penalty Defense Unit, who subsequently hired me as a forensic consultant.

As such, I was asked to develop a psychological assessment of Robinson's crimes, which I understood would be used to try to convince him to plead guilty and lead investigators to the bodies of three of his victims, Paula Godfrey, Lisa Stasi, and Catherine Clampitt.

I agreed to consult on this case in hopes of helping to bring closure to the families of these women. The thinking went that if Robinson cooperated, Evans and his unit might be able to negotiate a life sentence instead of the death penalty. Otherwise, if he went to trial and was found guilty, he was sure to get the death penalty and the bodies would remain missing. Ironically, for the first time in my life, my skills were being employed not to apprehend a serial killer, but to save his life.

Traditionally, a criminal profile is provided in unsolved cases, rather than a case in which the offender has already been detected, arrested, and charged. Therefore, most individuals who develop profiles are cautious about developing a psychological profile once the police have a suspect targeted.

My profile of John Robinson is different and should not be construed as a traditional offender profile. It is a post-secondary look at John Robinson's psychological behavior based on his crime scene actions and past criminal behavior; it is not a reconstruction of his crimes.

VICTIM	AGE	LURED BY	LOCATION OF BODY
1. LISA STASI	19	Job offer / Place to stay	Never Found
2. PAULA GODFREY	19	Job offer	Never Found
3. CATHERINE CLAMPIT	27	Job offer	Never Found
4. IZABELA K. LEWICKA	19	On-line	Barrel, Robinson's Rural farm
5. SUZETTE M. TROUTEN	27	On-line	Barrel, Robinson's rural farm
6. BEVERLY BONNER	49	Befriended when she worked in prison library	Storage Unit, Raymore, Missouri
7. SHEILA FAITH	51	Newspaper Ad	Storage Unit, Raymore, Missouri
8. DEBBIE FAITH	21	Newspaper Ad	Storage Unit, Raymore, Missouri

All crimes involve the acting out of criminal behavior in one form or another. In serial killings, this multitude of behaviors can be vividly expressed. *Vividly express* implies that the killer's actions, such as the use of a hammer, are observable compared to, for instance, the offender's intrinsic motives.

The vast majority of crimes that are profiled are serial murder, murder, serial sexual assaults, sexual assault/murder, and sexual assaults. This is because these offenses are "rich" in the display of an offender's criminal behavior and allow for a much clearer analysis to be made. The profile was developed based on information such as the following:

- SURVIVING VICTIMS AND WITNESS STATEMENTS
- CRIME SCENE REPORTS AND PHOTOGRAPHS
- MEDICAL EXAMINER'S REPORTS

- PSYCHOLOGICAL CLUES GLEANED FROM PERSONAL CORRE-
SPONDENCE WITH POTENTIAL VICTIMS, AND VICTIMS' FAMILY
MEMBERS

Contrary to popular opinion, modus operandi is not reliable for linking offenses. Disregarding an offense as the work of John Robinson solely on the basis of inconsistencies in his MO could be a big mistake and mislead investigators. An offender's MO can change over time as a result of a number of factors, especially experience.

When committing serial murder, this leads to refinements or changes in conduct so as to facilitate the completion of the crime. These refinements or changes can have a number of causes, chief among them victim's reponses to a killer's actions. For example, if the serial killer finds his victims resisting, he could incorporate a more deadly weapon to subdue the victim more quickly.

John Robinson's MO changed over time as a result of a number of factors such as the rise of the Internet. His MO was very dynamic and malleable and is not reliable for linking him to additional victims, although his signature behaviors are useful for linking him to other murders such as those of Catherine Clampitt, Paula Godfrey, and Lisa Stasi.

The "signature aspect" in a series of crimes is the behavior exhibited most commonly by violent, repeat offenders such as John Robinson. Signature behavior is also referred to as the offender's "calling card." It is an aspect of the offense that the offender acts out in fulfillment of psychological need. This may be manifested through particular verbal interaction with the victim, or through committing a series of actions on the victim in a particular order, and on each occasion.

One example of such victim interaction was John Robinson's use of several outlets to lure women, including newspaper ads and the Internet. The signature was the content of the ads used to attract the attention of women—not where they were placed. In the ads, Robinson claimed to be a wealthy businessman with international connections, luring women with offers of high-paying jobs and global travels. This is a signature.

Another signature was his habit of making contact with the family members of the victims in an attempt to reassure them as to the welfare of their missing family member. His intention was to deceive the family members into believing that their loved one was fine and enjoying herself on vacation.

Robinson's third signature that remained constant was that he had his victims sign and address correspondence to their families shortly before their deaths. He then would have the cards and letters sent from around different locations in North America and even overseas. For example, a longtime friend of John Robinson, Barbara Sandre, who lived in England at that time, received a letter from him asking her to mail some letters from Europe for his daughter, Kim. She mailed the two letters. The letters were sent to Sandre from Robinson already addressed, with return addresses in France and Switzerland. He wanted Kim's family to think that she was doing fine and having fun on her travels.

Profilers who attempt to link offenses believe that when these two aspects of offense behavior, that is, MO and signature, are used together, they can be effective in identifying linked crimes. I disagree. The problem with this hypothesis is that the MO and signature behavior may or may not be exhibited during the course of a crime, making them inconsistent for forensic behavioral purposes.

John Robinson had distinct behavioral themes, consistent in the ways that he went about luring and eventually killing his victims, that relate directly back to his behavior when not killing. This is referred to as John Robinson's *personal narrative*. The way in which Robinson treated women he did not kill was reflected in his behavior with those he did. For example, Alesia Cox testified that on one occasion, John Robinson became angry with her and threatened her while she was tied up and her arms were restrained. It is therefore likely that he became angry prior to killing his victims.

Another example of his personal narrative is the emotionally cold attitude that was reflected in an e-mail that he sent to Carolyn Trouten, mother of one of his victims. Carolyn Trouten testified that an e-mail from Robinson message appeared to have no emotion, no personality, as though it was written for a magazine.

MO AND SIGNATURE BEHAVIORS IN JOHN ROBINSON'S CRIMES

1. Con approach – wealthy businessman, offers of help, high-paying jobs and global travels (MO)
2. Methods of luring victims – Newspaper ads and Internet (signature)
3. Victims bludgeoned to death (MO)
4. Similar victimology – sex lifestyle, despondent women in need of financial help (MO)
5. Method of disposing victims' bodies (MO)
6. Slave contract – used in two murdered victims and numerous women who John Robinson did not kill (signature)
7. Made contact with victims' family/having others mail letters for him (signature)

John Robinson is a serial killer of an unusual sort. From all available sources, it appears that Robinson is the first individual ever sentenced to death who used the Internet to lure some of his victims. He had anonymity on the Internet, and thrill was achieved by seeking out unsuspecting strangers.

In regard to the number of victims, Robinson's crimes meet the standard, accepted definition of serial murder, that is, the killing of three or more victims over time, with a cooling off period in between. However, beyond this point is where some of his crimes and behaviors differ from most serial killers. This is not to say that he is not a serial killer but just different. The vexing part about Robinson's overall behavior is that his lifestyle had elements of sadistic sex and he was a murderer, too. A pressing question in this case is: did Robinson receive sexual sadistic pleasure from killing his victims?

In additional to the six murders that John Robinson was arrested and convicted of, he is suspected of two other murders, which would put his total number of victims at eight. Catherine Clampitt, Paula Godfrey, and Lisa Stasi's bodies have yet to be found. He was convicted of Lisa Stasi's murder. The typical U.S. serial killer has an average of eight victims, so in this one respect, Robinson is similar to other serial killers.

The ages of John Robinson's victims were somewhat similar to other serial killers' victims. At least in the U.S., serial killers prefer to target victims between the ages of eighteen and fifty years, with some exceptions. A study that I carried out on 107 serial killers found that only 3 percent of the offenders murdered teens. Three of John Robinson's victims, Lisa Stasi, Paula Godfrey, and Debbie Faith, were teenagers.

About one-half of all serial killers use some form of a ruse to lure victims, such as John Robinson did with the promise of a job and world travels. However, the typical serial killer usually murders his victims immediately, within hours after their abduction.

Rather than killing his victims immediately or holding them captive in a dungeon-like room as some sadistic serial killers do, John Robinson befriended his victims for some time prior to killing them.

He also made contact with some of the victims' parents. John Robinson's short-term and long-term intimate relationships with his victims and his contact with their family members departs significantly from the behavior of a typical serial killer, which is why some have hinted that he is not a true serial killer. Most serial killers murder strangers. My research on American serial killers found that over 80 percent of offender-victim relationships are stranger-to-stranger. When he first met them, Robinson's victims were strangers, but at the time of their deaths they certainly were not. In this regard, Robinson's relationship with his victims was similar to your typical intersexual homicides that involve some degree of intimacy between the offender and victim prior to the murder. So, in this sense Robinson's murders were typical of spousal or domestic-related homicides rather than serial killers who primarily killed strangers.

When Robinson's age is compared to other serial murderers a different picture emerges. John Robinson was fifty-six when he was first arrested for murder. My research found that the average age of serial killers is thirty at the time of their arrest, and that only 18 percent of serial killers are over the age of forty-two. Clearly, Robinson was older than the typical serial killer when he was arrested, which makes him even more unique.

Most serial killers have victims who are never known or accounted for by police. It is unlikely that the murder of Paula Godfrey in 1984 was John Robinson's first victim. At that time, he would have been around forty, which is old to start a career as a serial murderer. It is likely that John Robinson has victims who are unaccounted for dating back to the late 1970s and early 1980s. There is also a time gap between 1994 and 1999 during which he could have committed additional murders. Considering that three of Robinson's victims have never been found, it would not be surprising if he has killed and hid other victims.

Was John Robinson insane? Insanity is a legal term, not a medical term. To prove that John Robinson was insane, his criminal defense attorneys had to show that at the time of the commission of the serial killings, Robinson, as a result of a severe mental disease or defect, was unable to appreciate the nature, quality, and wrongfulness of his acts. In other words, he did not know right from wrong when he killed his victims. Without this ability to form willful criminal intent (*mens rea*), he cannot be held accountable for his crimes, the law argues, and he must be found not guilty by reason of insanity.

Robinson's defense attorneys, with the help of Dr. Dorothy Lewis, claimed that John Robinson suffered from a mental disease, including dissociation, emotional liability, and depression. Dr. Lewis, a noted child psychiatrist, interviewed John Robinson on September 7 and 9, 2002, and conducted interviews with some members of his immediate family. Dr. Lewis also reviewed some incomplete documentation then available on his mental and medical history.

I read her report. It indicates that Robinson had a history of severe physical and emotional abuse throughout childhood, resulting in episodic dissociate states. Dr. Lewis claimed that he lacked a rational understanding of the evidence and charges against him and had been unable to assist in his defense in any meaningful way.

The problem was, I was certain that John Robinson had manipulated the legal process by firing some of his attorneys and contriving conflicts with his attorneys, and by making it appear that he might attempt suicide. All these actions were merely a few of many rational and ongoing attempts to delay the trial he dreaded. All this, as well as the degree of planning prior to the murders and afterward, strongly suggested to me that Robinson was fully aware of his actions, and was totally responsible for his sadistic sexual behavior and the murders. It was not mental illness but rather his need to have power and control that drove him to seek domination over women.

John Robinson's desires do not fit the typical definition of a sadomasochist; there are no indications that he liked to play the masochist's role. Rather, John Robinson was totally into playing the sadist's role, which psychologically reflected his need to be in control.

Sexual sadism has a different origin from masochism. Sexual sadism was named by Richard von Krafft-Ebing after the Marquis de Sade, whose writings describe a pairing of sexual acts with domination, degradation, and violence. Those who only fantasize about sadistic sexual acts contrast dramatically with the viciousness of those sexually sadistic offenders who translate their fantasies into criminal actions.

Robinson fulfilled his sexual fantasies with willing partners but decided later that their lives were of no use and expendable. He saw his victims as mere objects. Robinson did not murder in order to achieve sadistic sexual gratification but rather through BDSM learned to depersonalize women, which allowed him to psychologically disassociate during the murders.

Although Robinson had a compulsion for sadism-related sexual activities, it is not clear that sadistic sex was an intentional motive for the murders. For sure, there were some women with whom he engaged in sadomasochistic sex but chose not to kill. The true motive behind why John Robinson lured some women from newspaper ads and the Internet is not clearly known. The motives could have been sex, murder, and, for at least three victims whom he pimped out, profit.

In psychological profiling terms, however, while each of the murders has separate elements, John Robinson's motives, while helpful to lawyers and jurors, are not necessarily required for profiling purposes. It is the individual differences between each of Robinson's offenses that are fruitful for developing a criminal profile.

I believe that Robinson did form a criminal intent to murder all his victims at some point after he befriended them. Profit was the direct motive for the murder of Lisa Stasi. Robinson had to murder Stasi in order to get rid of her so he could sell her infant daughter, Tiffany Stasi, to his brother, which he subsequently did. John Robinson wanted the exchange to appear like a legal adoption. Tiffany's mother was just in the way.

The consideration of victim selection, past criminal career, and various motives for the murders lays down a firm foundation: John Robinson clearly formed a criminal intent to commit murder. As such, he was not insane at the time of the murders and knew that his actions were wrong. Several actions on John Robinson's part support this theory.

For example, he concealed his crimes by placing five victims in barrels. This clearly shows that he intended to elude detection by hiding the evidence. Although Robinson concealed Suzette Trouten's and Izabela Lewicka's bodies in barrels, he did not go to great lengths to hide the barrels; the barrels were only found just a few yards behind his trailer in Linn County.

Robinson's sadistic behavior and murderous actions were a result of what may be called an excessive narcissism and an attitude toward women marked by feelings of superiority, disdain, and scorn. Examples of this view of other people in general and especially women are described below:

- SINCE I AM SO SUPERIOR, I AM ENTITLED TO SPECIAL TREATMENT AND PRIVILEGES
- I DON'T HAVE TO BE BOUND BY THE RULES THAT APPLY TO OTHER PEOPLE

- IF OTHERS DON'T RESPECT MY STATUS, THEY SHOULD BE PUNISHED
- OTHER PEOPLE SHOULD SATISFY MY NEEDS
- OTHER PEOPLE SHOULD RECOGNIZE HOW SPECIAL I AM
- NO ONE'S NEEDS SHOULD INTERFERE WITH MY OWN

His demand that women be passive and powerless was seen as an entitlement. Robinson's power over women was a kind of psychological euphoria or rush that he sought to maintain at all times but in reality could not. The need for sexual domination and control over women eventually took precedence over his greed. His attempt to maintain this euphoria accounted for his repeated deceptions and murders.

For example, in Robinson's first known murder, his motive appears to be profit as demonstrated by him selling Lisa Stasi's daughter, whereas the motive in his later murders is not clear. Robinson's psychological need to fuse sex with aggression did not suddenly surface one day. Rather, it had been building up and in the past had been satisfied only by swindling money through cons. However, Robinson's behavior escalated. Masochism—pain, bondage, and humiliation—was used as a vehicle to help him achieve a fantasized escape from reality. He actually felt inferior to others, which accounts for his narcissism. Consequently, Robinson's use of vulnerable women and the need for a continual fantasized reality turned into violent murder.

The thrill and psychological rush that Robinson achieved by deceiving others out of money was no longer enough. He began to distort and fuse aggression, deception, and rough sex. He could not conceptualize others as separate individuals, but as extensions of his conceptual self-representations—something or someone to control. His psychological need progressed to having non-intimate contact with an object—a possession.

For example, some people find that they are sexually impotent unless they use a fixated fetish such as a shoe, or are wearing certain clothing, or using someone as a possession. The compulsion to have any female as an object of possession consumed John Robinson. He turned his ability from conning others out of their money to luring women with clever ruses. For Robinson, it was a natural transition.

He told Barbara Sandre, who had known him for almost four decades, that he had never married and had four adopted children. Of course, he lied. Robinson had four biological children, born to him and his wife of thirty-eight years, Nancy. He also told Sandre that he worked for the CIA. The lengths to which Robinson went in order to lure women to Kansas was extreme and showed a true distortion of reality.

Robinson lived his life as a form of a story, with himself at center stage. Life stories like his are intimately connected to behavior such as murder, behavior that is outside of socially approved boundaries. Robinson's victims were perceived as fitting in with an internalized object, a visual image in Robinson's mind that was both a desperately pursued and a hatefully unwanted fantasized person.

Robinson sought the one thing that he hated—women. His hatred of women could have derived from poor past relationships with women. Whether the relationships were real or fantasized is not important—for Robinson the feelings of hate, anger, and rage were real.

And yet there is no history that John Robinson's criminal behavior was influenced by early childhood traumatic relationships, as suggested by Dr. Lewis, or, for that matter, Sigmund Freud. Robinson's personality relied on a *self-verification* process through which he used others to verify his self-image—a way to maintain control of his life and others around him. Thus, Robinson adopted life strategies that elicit self-confirmatory feedback from the women that he interacted with. Unfortunately, that feedback was not enough.

It is important to understand the nature of Robinson's overall behavior. He was a thief and the ultimate con man. He lived his entire adult life creating business scams in order to defraud people out of their hard-earned money. He accomplished this by setting up various fraudulent companies as a way to lure investors and make the investors believe that they would make a profit.

A successful con for Robinson gave him thrill-seeking sensations. Each successful con fed Robinson's appetite to maintain control over his crumbing life. Obtaining money by way of cons was for Robinson like the feeling a crack addict gets from the drug; the more cons he did the higher the psychological rush. It's like skiing off of a seven-thousand-foot cliff with no parachute—you suddenly find that you need more and more thrills to achieve the euphoria. Murder became Robinson's new drug.

Robinson's behavior that eventually led to murder derived from his personal psychology of being a manipulative individual, which was formed early in life and focused on selfish personal gain. Psychologically, the thrill for him in carrying out a successful con was not in the obtainment of money but rather the rush of thinking that he had outsmarted someone. He developed this impersonal attitude early on. One investor commented about Robinson years before the murders, saying "he made a very good impression, well-dressed, nice-looking, late twenties, seemed to know a lot, very glib, good speaker." He was self-assured, exhibited controlling and calculating behavior throughout his life as demonstrated by the previous comments. He was able to isolate his emotional rage from his cognitive thoughts, which allowed him to develop a view of himself as impervious to future rejection. This "dismissing style" personality aided his development into an emotionally cold serial killer.

He viewed his victims as nothing more than an object to be abused for pleasure, as demonstrated by his repeated need for impersonal sex. Normal relationships were difficult for Robinson. He was not aware of his loneliness and self-hatred because he was so self-absorbed, which caused him to transfer anger and hate onto his victims; more important, his self-absorption played a major role in his inability to have empathy for others. Robinson mastered the style of maintaining superficial relationships with others, which is why it was easy for him to lure victims into his web using cons and ploys. The dismissing-type killers hold a view of themselves and others that downplays the importance of everyday attachment relationships and which relates back to the need to maintain felt security as previously mentioned. A dismissing personality type, Robinson used his superficial persona to depersonalize women. I feel that this form of depersonalization was carried over into murder.

Depersonalization in this regard was a way of denying the emotionality of the other person by treating her as though she were an object. This type of behavior is referred to as reification, the ability only to look at a person as an object of interest. In other words, Robinson was always emotionally and psychologically detached from his victims. This detachment does not mean that he was not aware of what he was doing. Rather, due to his detachment Robinson used sadistic identification, his cold and detached attitude, to transform the seeking of relations based upon affectional need into relations based upon power, dominance, and submission. In everyday behavior, Robinson was impersonal and dismissive of other people in his personal life; however, in the way in which he dealt with his victims during and after the murders, he actually displayed a high degree of personal attachment.

A serial killer with this kind of personality is likely to spend more time with the body or revisit his crime scenes, which could be why Robinson chose to keep two barrels containing victims behind his trailer. Hiding Izabela Lewicka and Suzette Trouten's bodies only yards from his trailer may have been his way of maintaining control over his fantasized objects, possibly to satisfy his instrumental goal—voyeuristic sexual gratification.

This fantasizing most likely occurred due to the longing to continue to control the victims, to denigrate them as objects even in death. The fact that his trailer in Linn County was an hour's drive from his permanent residence makes no difference. Serial killers often travel hundreds of miles to revisit their crime scenes or victims' graves. It is estimated that Lewicka's body had been in the barrel almost a year and Trouten's body around three months. He had had ample time to dispose of the victims in another location.

Other behaviors could suggest he attempted to relive his crimes. For example, during their search of Robinson's home and locker B16 at Needmor Storage in Olathe, Kansas, investigators found many items that belonged to Suzette Trouten. Among her personal items were crystal items, knickknacks, a brass unicorn figurine, a textbook, a Mickey Mouse watch, jewelry, and two jewelry boxes. He also gave some victims' personal belongings to other women as gifts, which is a behavior often displayed by serial killers.

Barbara Sandre testified that John Robinson gave her bedding, an oil painting, three hundred to four hundred books, and an antique mortar and pestle. These items were later identified as belonging to Izabela Lewicka. Historically, serial killers such as John Robinson have typically experienced previous intense childhood family conflicts. These conflicts fuel the killer's attitude of distrust toward the world quite early in life.

It is unlikely that a full account of Robinson's childhood experiences will ever come to light, especially because his mother is dead.

Robinson has said that his childhood lacked intimacy but that he was never abused. He also appeared to have had a fairly normal childhood. But it is likely that Robinson's fear of being rejected developed as a young adult. Interviews with convicted serial killers have revealed a hatred of women for wrongs they believe women have done to them in the past. It is possible that Robinson experienced traumatic rejections from former girlfriends or women he fantasized about. To compensate for his fear of rejection he developed a narcissistic attitude.

He saw confident women as overly powerful and a threat. He had disdain for these types of women, but was also both attracted to and fearful of them. There were some women whom Robinson conned, deceived, and engaged in sex with but chose not to kill. Perhaps some of the surviving victims were more inquisitive and displayed self-confidence, which may have signalled to him that they would resist his aggression.

Based on my analysis of 300,000 pages of case files on John Robinson's crimes, I classified him as a cognitive-object serial killer. His pre- and post-aggressive behavior was calm and calculated, which defines the cognitive aspect of the serial murder classification. Robinson's view and treatment of his victims manifested itself in the form of seeing the women as merely objects, props to use and abuse, some even sadistically, as he wished. Anything and anyone encountered by John Robinson was seen as a means to an end. In the end, he was a master of nothing but the plight of his life— death.

On January 21, 2003, Robinson was sentenced to death in Kansas. He was quietly transferred to a small solitary cell at the El Dorado Correctional Facility outside of Wichita, where he awaits execution. To avoid the death penalty in Missouri and save his family the embarrassment of another trial, Robinson pleaded guilty to the murders of Beverly Bonner, Sheila and Debbie Faith, Paula Godfrey, and Catherine Clampitt.

The whereabouts of Lisa Stasi, Paula Godfrey, and Catherine Clampitt remain a mystery.

CHAPTER 9

THE BATON ROUGE
SERiAL KiLLER

GINI GREEN WAS A devoted and caring nurse. It was out of character for her to be late for work at HCS Infusion Network on Picardy Avenue in Baton Rouge.

About midmorning on September 24, 2001, one of Green's coworkers became concerned over her absence and decided to drive over to Green's Stanford Avenue home to check on her. That's when the coworker found Green dead in bed with the sheet pulled up around her neck. The autopsy later confirmed that Green had been sexually assaulted and died of asphyxiation due to strangulation at about 9:00 A.M., September 24.

There were no signs that someone had forced his way inside, which helped fuel the rumor that Green was killed by a repairman who had worked in her house. Detectives said the motive for Green's murder was not robbery, although several valuables were missing. Police discovered that the killer had stolen Green's cloth purse and Nokia cellular phone, which was later found across town in an industrial area. Her purse was never found. While there were no immediate suspects, whoever the killer was, he left his DNA at the crime scene, inside Green's body.

Back in the neighborhood where Green had lived, Charlotte Pace, a twenty-two-year-old graduate student at Louisiana State University, was worried. She lived with two roommates at 2107 Stanford Avenue, just three doors down from Green's residence. Although Pace did not know Gini Green, she was frightened when her neighbor was found slain and had expressed fears to her mother, Ann Pace.

Eight months after the murder, Pace finally decided to move several miles away to South Baton Rouge, a safe and popular location for LSU college students. Her move was only temporary—she had accepted a job in Atlanta with Deloitte & Touche. However, Charlotte Pace's dream was cut short on May 31, 2002.

Two days after moving from her Stanford Avenue address to a townhouse at 1211 Sharlo Avenue, she was found stabbed to death. Face up with her blouse and her bra pushed up and her pants down around her ankles; a roommate discovered her body at about 2 P.M. An LSU student who lived across the street from the Sharlo Avenue townhouses said that Pace's roommate ran out of the apartment screaming and crying, yelling for the police and an ambulance.

Police investigators found a ghastly scene at the Pace residence. Blood was everywhere, especially in the kitchen. As in the Green case, she had been sexually assaulted. It was all in the police report; Pace's half-nude body was found beaten and riddled with eighty-one stab and puncture wounds from a flathead screwdriver and a knife. She was found on her roommate's bedroom floor, with her eyes swollen nearly shut, her hair bloodied, and her hands bruised as though she had fought her attacker. It was obvious that Pace had put up a fierce struggle, perhaps even injuring her killer.

When crime scene investigators searched Pace's townhouse they discovered several personal items missing. According to police reports, Pace's brown and tan Louis Vuitton wallet with keys to her

BMW were missing. The killer also had stolen her cordless phone handset and a silver ring. However, the police lucked out; the killer left behind two key forensic clues—DNA evidence and a Rawlings tennis shoe print.

Police backtracked her movements. Pace had left work around noon to prepare for a friend's wedding. Stopping at home first for lunch, she went and sat on the couch, watching TV, enjoying a sandwich and Diet Dr Pepper. Afterward, her half-eaten sandwich and three grapes were found on the couch, undisturbed, suggesting that she was interrupted when she went to answer the door.

The MO appeared to be the same as the Green murder: no signs of forced entry. The killer must have used a ruse to get Pace to open the door. The risks were just too high for a scorned boyfriend or some other acquaintance to be the killer.

Only a few yards separated each townhouse, and neighbors could likely identify a regular visitor. The killer was a stranger who stalked his victim—watching Pace come and go—and eventually following her from Stanford Avenue to her new residence on Sharlo.

Just a few days after Pace's murder, four neighbors told police about a light-skinned black man they had seen watching her townhouse in the hours preceding her murder. No official police composite sketch of this person of interest (POI) was done. Rather, the witnesses worked with a volunteer who, at her own expense, used the same software police use to develop their composites. The POI sketch was submitted to police, but was never publicly released. The composite ended up being put out like a flyer on car windshields and made a brief appearance on the Internet before disappearing.

In August 2002, three months after the Charlotte Pace murder, Police Chief Pat Englade of Baton Rouge decided to form a task force to track down the killer. The purpose of the task force was to establish lines of inquiry between West Baton Rouge and the three incorporated communities in East Baton Rouge Parish, as well as the FBI and the Louisiana state police. It all sounded good on paper, but reality was another thing.

The Baton Rouge task force at first did not connect the two murders. They said publicly that there were too many differences for there to be a connection. For example, Green was strangled and left in her bed while Pace fought her killer and suffered repeated stab wounds. The task force mentality was probably best summed up in a report by a detective who was about as tuned in as Inspector Clouseau: "The rage in the Pace homicide is totally different from what we saw in the Gina Green homicide."

Unlike the Baton Rouge task force, I sought out additional evidence that there was indeed a serial killer targeting women in Baton Rouge. I compared the characteristics of female murders in Louisiana to the current unsolved murders and to the sixty-plus unsolved female murders that had occurred in Baton Rouge over the last decade. Then, I examined the national crime figures for the years 1998 to 2002.

When compared to other states, Louisiana consistently ranked in the top five for males who murdered females in single incidents. So, in this one sense, the Baton Rouge murders were no different from female murders statewide. However, the crime statistics also showed that females in Louisiana tended to be murdered by males they knew, who acted alone. The crimes of the Baton Rouge serial killer just didn't fit your typical female murder pattern in the state.

I had been following the case closely. Although DNA analysis later linked the Green and Pace murders to one killer, the task force was reluctant to use the "SK" word—serial killer. My research on 107 known American serial killers pointed out similarities in the Green and Pace murders. Beyond the obvious similarly that both victims were sexually assaulted, there was other elements linking the murders.

The murders were committed indoors with no forced entry. The murders were committed during daylight hours, which suggested that either the killer was unemployed or worked nights. The victims' purses and phones were missing, which suggested a slight similarity. For me, though, it was the geography of the Green and Pace crimes that pointed to a *Viper* serial killer.

Vipers are serial killers who lay low and attack in the same area. They don't venture out very far to attack and dump their victims. Selecting Pace as a victim was more than coincidence. Before she moved, Pace was Green's neighbor—they were *connected*. Once I knew that, I knew that there was trouble in Baton Rouge.

After the Pace murder, I began to map the Baton Rouge serial killer's geographical behavior. I plotted four locations in my Predator profiling system: Gini Green's home address, the address where her cell phone was found, Pace's townhouse on Sharlo Avenue, and Pace's previous address on Stanford. These four locations were just a start; I needed more crime locations before a clear pattern could emerge.

Unfortunately, there wasn't long to wait.

Pam Kinamore, forty-two, an interior designer, was last seen at her Denham Springs, Louisiana, antiques store, Comfort and Joys, around 9 P.M. on July 12, 2002. Byron Kinamore, Pam's husband, called police when he arrived home just before midnight and saw that her car was there but she was not.

In the upscale Briarwood Place subdivision, police found little to go on at the home of Byron and Pamela Kinamore. The car in the driveway suggested that Kinamore made it home that night. There was water in the bathtub, as if she was getting set to take a bath when someone or something interrupted her. A fast food cup had been set on the edge of the tub, keys left in the back door. Most telling, a small drop of blood was found at the foot of her bed.

Considered all together, the physical evidence suggested that Pam Kinamore had been getting ready to take a bath when she was confronted by the killer in the bedroom. In some way, he had then overpowered her and taken her with him. Police searched around the clock trying to find her.

They conducted aerial searches around the Airline Highway neighborhood. The Kinamore family plastered flyers with Kinamore's photo, description, and a contact number around Baton Rouge.

While the cops investigated and came up with nothing, the Baton Rouge murders had become national news. I was asked to appear on MSNBC and Fox News in July 2002 to give a profile of the Baton Rouge serial killer. Using the Gini Green and Charlotte Pace crime sites, plus Pam Kinamore's abduction location, I carried out the first geographical profiling analysis of the Baton Rouge serial murders.

The profile that I provided MSNBC and Fox News was specific. I predicted that the serial killer would lay low for several months, and when he struck again his crimes would be displaced to another region. In the map on the opposite page, I predicted that the serial killer had an anchor point located between the College-town, College Hills, and Arlington areas in south Baton Rouge. The anchor point, I stressed, could be the killer's home, girlfriend's home, work, or parents' home. I also pointed out that the killer would likely dump future victims in water or remote woods in hopes of destroying DNA evidence. This guy was learning as he went along. He was becoming *forensically aware*.

GEOGRAPHICAL PROFILE OF BATON ROUGE SERIAL KILLER

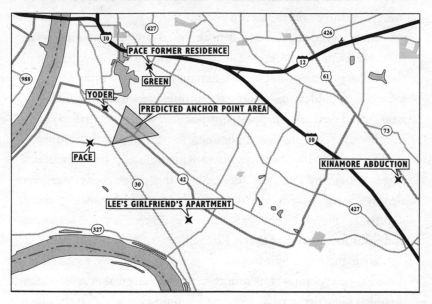

On July 16, four days after Kinamore was abducted, Joseph Breaux, a member of a state surveying crew, saw what he thought was a mannequin lying in a washout on the bank of the Whiskey Bay Pilot Channel off Interstate 10 in Iberville Parish. Soon, he realized it was a partially decomposed woman's body, floating facedown in the stagnant water. The autopsy later confirmed that it was the body of Pam Kinamore.

Cause of death was a cut throat; she had bled out. She had also been sexually assaulted. Despite little forensic evidence at the Kinamore crime scene, which the police now took to be the woman's bedroom from which she was abducted, the killer made the same mistake that he had in the Green and Pace murders—he left his

DNA on the victim. In fact, in all the autopsies to date, semen had been found in or on the victim's body.

Once again, the killer did nothing to prevent his own body from betraying him.

Geographical profiling is a dynamic process. As more crime locations are added to Predator, the profile is modified, resulting in a new predicted anchor point and possible wider or smaller police search area. Knowing that, I obtained the geographical coordinates of the Whiskey Bay location where Kinamore was discovered and entered them in Predator. Along with the other crime locations already in the system, the new profile shifted the anchor point slightly to the northwest, which was expected, since Kinamore's body was found west of Baton Rouge.

With the three murders linked to one killer, my second predicted anchor point was just south of the College Lakes area, which included Gourrier Avenue. Because I had no evidence that the killer had followed Kinamore home from her business in Denham Springs, her work location was not included in my first or second profile.

Meanwhile, the police were stumped about how the killer was eluding detection and gaining entry into the victims' homes. During a later visit to the Kinamore crime scene, my attention was immediately drawn to the privacy fence that separated their backyard from an open field where new houses were expected to be built in the near future. I was able to walk up to the fence and peep over with a clear view of the back of the Kinamore home. While there's no evidence that the serial killer ever parked in the woods behind the fence, I knew that this secluded area could have provided him with a perfect hiding place and staging area for the eventual assault on Kinamore in her bedroom.

* * *

Trineisha Dené Colomb was a twenty-three-year-old with a bright future. A former U.S. Army soldier, she liked military life and planned to join the Marine Corps Reserves. On November 21, 2002, she decided to visit her mother's grave in Grand Coteau, near Lafayette. Colomb, twenty-three, last spoke to her family around 12:30 P.M. Her family reported her missing on November 22.

Late in the day on the twenty-first, a resident near Grand Coteau in St. Landry Parish noticed a black 1994 Mazda MX3 parked on Robbie Road. When the car was still there the next morning, the resident phoned the sheriff's department. Responding investigators found Colomb's car sitting on the side of the road with the car facing the direction that indicated she was leaving. Inside, police found her car keys, coin purse, driver's license, and nothing else. Three days after her abandoned car was found, a rabbit hunter found Colomb's body in a wooded area about three hundred yards off Renaud Drive in the town of Scott, Louisiana. Scott is about twenty miles from where Colomb's car was discovered.

The autopsy on Colomb's body suggested that she vigorously fought off her attacker. She had also been sexually assaulted. One month after her body was found in Scott, the Baton Rouge task force announced that DNA found in the Colomb murder matched DNA in the Green, Pace, and Kinamore murders. Colomb was the killer's first known black victim.

As I predicted, the serial killer aborted for several months and dumped the body in remote woods. I plotted the two crime locations associated with Colomb's murder, her abduction site and the site were her body was found twenty miles away in Scott.

My analysis using locations associated with all four of the linked murders shifted the predicted police search and killer's home area. What this meant was that previous geographical profiles produced by Predator were no longer relevant because new crimes had been added to the analysis.

I wondered if the serial killer really would commit these risky murders at the victims' homes in an area in which he lives? Could the killer live further east, maybe south or possibly north of Baton Rouge? But there was no evidence to suggest that he lived in these directions. Geographical profiling is based solely on known crime locations. Did I know of *all* of the crimes committed by this serial killer?

All the locations relevant to the four unsolved murders were entered in Predator. The results predicted two new anchor points. That was unusual. The first anchor point was in Baton Rouge near the West Lakeshore Drive community; the second point was anchored in Port Allen, just across the Mississippi River from Baton Rouge.

Early in February 2003, I received an e-mail from a person calling himself Allan Scott. Scott told me that he could not reveal his true identity due to fear of losing his job. Considering the attitude of the task force, I completely understood where he was coming from. And while I was suspicious, Scott had information about the task force investigation not known to the public that only a member of the task force could know.

I gave Scott my geographical profiles and my criminal profile suggesting that the serial killer was black. Scott would later tell me that he was using my geographical profiles to track down the serial killer, but the profiles were not being used by the task force as a whole. Scott said that there was no way the task force would buy into my profile that the killer was black.

At a task force news conference after my profile was sent to Scott, they announced the release of a "partial" psychological profile of the serial killer developed by FBI profilers. According to the task force, the purpose of releasing the profile was on the chance that someone would recognize a person that might fit the profile. The task force said that the FBI profile predicted that the killer was somewhere between twenty-five and thirty-five years of age and white. However, after the murders were solved, the FBI profilers claimed that their profile did not state the serial killer's suspected race. In all my years of reading criminal profiles, I've never seen the race of the perpetrator omitted in a report.

I find it hard to believe that the FBI profile stated the offender's approximate shoe size but did not consider his race. I have no doubt that the FBI profilers profiled the Baton Rouge serial killer as white, like they always do, which was reinforced by eyewitness accounts of the alleged perpetrator.

Investigators in the field like to have some direction from profilers about who they are searching for. If there is no racial distinction made, detection becomes impossible. My analysis had told me that there was a high probability the killer was black, with a lengthy criminal history including burglary. Experience in burglaries allows serial killers to become comfortable with entering victims' homes. I was sure this one was a Viper, with juvenile convictions and a history of voyeuristic activities.

I made several more formal attempts to contact the task force to offer my profiling advice pro bono; I never received a reply. Their lack of response was par for the course. During the course of the investigation, Chief of Police Pat Englade turned down help from other criminal profilers including Dr. Robert Keppel, even over the objection of some victims' family members.

The killer was still out there, ready to kill again.

CHAPTER **10**

TOMBSTONE TERRiTORY

AT JUST ABOUT THE same time in February 2003 that I received the e-mail from the task force detective surreptitiously seeking my assistance, I got a phone call from detectives in Zachary, Louisiana, just twenty-four miles north of Baton Rouge.

The two detectives from Zachary were looking into two cold case homicides. They wanted me to help solve them. But before we could get into it, they were suddenly pulled off the case. A new investigator took over; he wasn't interested in any profile, geographical or otherwise.

I finally got my "in" when a concerned citizens group in Baton Rouge invited me to come to town and look at how unique these murders were, and to give a presentation about my profiles.

Fear hung heavy in the stagnant air over the Louisiana bayous. When I got to Baton Rouge in May 2003, I saw firsthand how scared women were. Homemade flyers pinned to trees across the city known as "Red Stick" warned: "Killer on the loose." Community members were marching on the capitol to express their fears.

I was given a guided tour by the current renters at the Sharlo Avenue location where Pace was murdered. Scanning the environmental layout of the complex, I knew that this killer was an experienced criminal with a history of burglary. The front of the townhouses at Sharlo Avenue all faced each other, making it easy to witness someone at the front door. In the back of the townhouse was the garage surrounded by a privacy fence, which could have provided the killer a safe way to enter the residence without being seen.

I later visited the area where Colomb was abducted as part of my crime scene investigation. The cemetery behind St. Charles Church where Colomb went to visit her mother, Verna's, grave is separated only by a pasture. As I stood next to the Colomb headstone, which reads, "I lay next to my mother joining her as an angel in heaven," an eerie feeling came over me. Dené Colomb had been visiting her mother's grave the day she was abducted and murdered, and she is now buried at the very same place.

A dirt path leads from St. Charles Church to Robbie Road, where Colomb's car was found. There's one way in and out of Robbie Road. A white house built in the French colonial style sits at one end of the dead-end road. It's isolated and hidden by tall trees and bushes. Robbie Road can't be seen from the main highway. Because it was daylight, the killer needed a victim who was alone in a secluded area. The location provided him a safety net to carry out the abduction without being witnessed.

During the twenty-mile ride from Grand Coteau to Renaud Drive to visit the Colomb crime scene area, I realized that this serial killer did not randomly pick the remote body dump location in Scott. He had to be very familiar with the area to know the route. Either he lived or worked in the area or had family who lived in the area.

Once on Renaud Drive, I traveled about a fourth of a mile until I approached a curve in the road. In the bend of the curve, on the left, was a path just wide enough for a vehicle to pass over. Across the road was a small white house. I thought, this guy must be confident as hell to carry a victim to this location in daylight with a house just across the street.

I drove across the narrow path that entered a small grassy clearing about fifty yards long by thirty yards wide. Getting out of the car, I noticed an opening in the woods directly in front of me that was overgrown with weeds. "This is the path the killer carried Dené Colomb's body down," I thought to myself.

To the left of the path sat a tree. I saw a camouflaged wooden box attached to the bottom. On closer inspection, I recognized the box as an instant camera, the kind that deer hunters often use to take photos of an area to see if deer visit the location. In today's high-tech society, the task force was using an instant camera to try to catch a devious serial killer.

It probably seems odd to say that I had a feeling that whoever was killing people in Baton Rouge had done it someplace else nearby. After all, while psycho-geographic profiling is an inexact science, it is a science nonetheless, one that relies more on inductive rather than deductive reasoning.

Serial killers operate within a specific killing territory, the wedge discussed earlier. But the coordinates that Predator uses to form the wedge are based on information known at the time the information is input, and then updated as crimes occur. The operative word here is "known." There could be other crimes committed by the same killer nearby, across town, across continents. It always pays to start close to home. And so, in February 2003, I determined to test a hypothesis: that the Baton Rouge killer had also operated in nearby communities.

Using my profile of the Baton Rouge serial killer, I discovered the two similar murders that had occurred years earlier in Zachary, again, only twenty-four miles from Baton Rouge. They were the same two the Zachary cops had called me about. Just on distance alone, not even knowing if the murders were similar, Zachary should have been part of the task force hunting the LA serial killer.

I was sure that I had stumbled upon a possible link between the Baton Rouge killings and the two cold case murders in Zachary.

Two weeks before she was murdered, divorcee Connie Warner phoned police to report a prowler outside her house on Job Street in the Zachary Oak Shadows subdivision. No one thought much about it. Then Warner's daughter, Tracy, a teenager at the time, arrived home around 9 P.M. on April 23, 1992. After a weekend out, Tracy could not find her mother. Since her mother couldn't see to drive at night, Tracy thought it was odd she wasn't home.

After waiting for two and a half hours, Tracey became worried enough to call her grandfather. When he came over, they searched the house, found blood spatter, and called the police. Warner, forty-one, had disappeared. Two weeks later, a truck driver found Connie Warner's body in a ditch near Capitol Lake in Baton Rouge. Naked, her body was well into decomposition. Examining the body, a Zachary Police Department detective surmised that Warner had been strangled.

Back at her house, police found no evidence of forced entry. But they did find evidence that Warner had struggled with her attacker. Police found droplets of blood, her bed messed up, and overturned furniture, clearly signs of a violent struggle. Forensic specialists at the crime scene collected bedsheets and towels but never tested them for DNA.

A search of Warner's car found evidence that the killer had driven her to Baton Rouge and returned it later to the victim's carport. Police also found evidence that someone had vomited in the back seat but no forensic analysis was ever done of this evidence either. In fact, it could have been the killer's vomit, for all the police knew.

Police were baffled. How did the killer gain entry to Warner's home? Did she open the door to her attacker? Why would a killer park his car and drive the victim's vehicle to get rid of the body, then return it to her home? If the killer parked his car in the Oak Shadows subdivision, that would be risky, considering that several police officers lived there. Maybe the killer didn't know this. At the time, police had no immediate suspects in Warner's abduction and murder.

Not long after the Warner murder in April 1993, fifteen-year-old Michelle Chapman and her boyfriend were attacked in a Zachary cemetery by a machete-wielding fiend. The attacker fled and dropped his weapon in the rain after a police officer happened upon the scene. Based upon eyewitness descriptions, Zachary police made a sketch of a black male. Until the case was featured on *America's Most Wanted*, no progress was made.

Whether you agree with his politics or not, there is no denying that John Walsh's *America's Most Wanted* is effective at catching "bad guys." After the case was featured in a reenactment, a tip sent to the show led Zachary police to a local man named Derrick Todd Lee. Lee, who had a juvenile record for burglary, rode through Zachary's neighborhoods on his bicycle. Interestingly enough, the cemetery where the machete attack occurred was directly behind the Oak Shadows subdivision near Warner's home.

In 1996, Lee was picked out of a lineup by witnesses for the machete attack. Unfortunately, it was too late. The statute of limitations on the machete assault had run out. Then in 1997, the Zachary Police Department received numerous complaints about a Peeping Tom hanging out in the Oak Shadows neighborhood. Derrick Lee was identified by police as the person of interest in the Peeping Tom incidents.

However, police never followed up on Lee's involvement in the cemetery attack, and if they made a link between Derrick Todd Lee and the Warner murder, they kept it to themselves. At the very least, experience should have alerted investigators that the Warner murder and the machete attack were linked, if based on nothing other than the proximity of the two crimes.

On April 19, 1998, neighbors noticed a little boy playing alone at 1721 Saul Avenue, which is near the Oak Shadows subdivision. The boy, then three years old, told the neighbor his mother was "lost." The neighbor entered Randi Mebruer's home and saw signs of a violent struggle. Mebruer, twenty-eight, a home health care nurse, had vanished from her Zachary home during the night of April 18.

Zachary police were immediately dispatched to the Mebruer address. Upon arrival, they found evidence of a struggle and bloody garbage bags under the carport. Randi Mebruer was nowhere to be found. Detectives figured the killer used the garbage bags to wrap Mebruer's body up before he moved her from the residence during the night.

Forensic specialists worked the crime scene, bagging evidence, looking for fingerprints, organic matter, anything that would lead them to Mebruer's abductor. Once again, the Zachary police failed to follow through on immediate DNA tests. Instead, they waited until five years later in 2003 before doing that.

From the beginning, Zachary police considered Mebruer's husband, Mike Mebruer, the prime suspect. While it would not be surprising if Randi Mebruer knew her killer, since the majority of homicide victims do, the Louisiana Attorney General's Office took the unusual step of stating publicly that they thought Mike Mebruer had killed his wife. Mebruer's body was not recovered and remains missing to this day.

* * *

I sent a message to my contact on the task force expressing my belief that the cold case Zachary murders were linked to the Baton Rouge killings. But the task force would have none of it. They chose to ignore the Zachary murders because DNA didn't link the crimes. It didn't, of course, because the DNA evidence in the unsolved Zachary homicides had never been tested, despite the fact that the evidence was available at the time for such testing by the Baton Rouge cops.

This ignorance would cost the life of another bright young woman. Carrie Yoder, twenty-six, was alone on the night of March 3, 2003, in her small but comfortable house on Dodson Avenue just off the LSU campus. Yoder was a PhD student in ecology at Louisiana State University. She was last seen around 7:45 P.M. on the day she disappeared; Yoder was working on a presentation for her course work at LSU.

Just as with the previous victims of the Baton Rouge serial killer, police found no forced entry at Yoder's house. Oddly, there didn't appear to be anyone home when Carrie Yoder's boyfriend, Lee Stanton, went to the Dodson Avenue house the next day to check on her. Stanton said it didn't make sense that Carrie would open the door to a stranger, considering that he had installed a peephole in her front door only months before she went missing.

Only one item appeared to be out of place in the Yoder house a key holder that was on the wall next to the front door. It was hanging to one side, as though it was almost knocked off the wall.

Ten days after Carrie Yoder disappeared, a fisherman found her naked body floating in Whiskey Bay about three-quarters of a mile from a boat launch under Interstate 10. This location was near where Pam Kinamore's body was found. East Baton Rouge coroner Louis Cataldie determined that Yoder had been strangled and beaten. She had also been sexually assaulted.

When a body is submerged in water over a ten day period, it usually accelerates decomposition. Skin slippage occurs, with the skin literally slipping off the body as it decomposes. Luckily, Yoder's body had been submerged during a period when the water was cool. The elements had conspired to make sure that there was DNA evidence still left in the body.

The autopsy revealed that the killer left his DNA, just has he had done in the previous four murders. Several weeks after Yoder's body was found, DNA analysis confirmed that Yoder's killer was the same person who had killed the previous four victims. The Baton Rouge serial killer had stuck again.

Even before the DNA analysis came back linking the Yoder murder to the previous four murders, I knew that the Yoder murder was the work of the same guy.

After lying low for several months after the Colomb murder, the killer had gained enough confidence to move his attacks back to his comfort zone of Baton Rouge. Carrying out another murder back in his comfort zone was a reflection that the task force was not doing a particularly good job. Otherwise, the killer would have displaced his crimes even further away from Baton Rouge. The Yoder murder location was right in the heart of the zone where Predator had said that the killer lived.

The fact that the killer returned to his previous hunting ground was, however, vexing. On the one hand I felt that this confirmed what my analysis was saying. On the other hand, I was somewhat apprehensive about the notion that the serial killer would take such a risk. Other than the possible linkage of the Warner and Mebruer murders, no additional murders at that time had been linked to the Baton Rouge serial killer.

I entered two crime locations related to the Carrie Yoder murder into Predator. Predator predicted that the police search should be anchored east of Highway 61 around the Emmett Bourgeois Lane. This was the final geographical profile that I developed in the Baton Rouge serial murders.

Finally, in late May 2003, Derrick Todd Lee was finally identified by police as the suspected Baton Rouge serial killer. Lee voluntarily provided his DNA to the state to compare against he DNA recovered from the victims. Before he could be officially charged, Lee left town, headed for Atlanta. Eluding police several times over a period of a week, Lee was finally arrested without incident while poking around a tire shop in southwest Atlanta. From the Fulton County Jail in Atlanta, he was extradited to Baton Rouge. Police launched an extensive investigation into Lee's background. As I predicted in my profile, they found that Lee was a high school dropout and unskilled laborer who had held numerous construction jobs.

Between April 1982 and July 1993 Derrick Todd Lee had been charged and convicted four times with burglary. He would subsequently use his burglary experience to gain entry to his murder victims' homes. In June 1996, Lee was convicted of two counts of voyeuristic activity in Calcasieu Parish. Receiving two years probation, a $200 fine, and court costs, he was ordered to stay away from the victim. After that slap on the wrist, in November 1997, Lee was arrested again as a Peeping Tom. This time, the Zachary court sentenced him to pay a fine of $414 and court costs or serve nine days in jail. He was placed on probation for two years.

Lee was a burglarizing voyeur, the type of person I predicted he would be. To get a clear perspective of the geographical profiles developed, I have listed below the geographical profiling results. It is important to remember that a new geographical analysis is required for each new crime:

ORDER OF GEOGRAPHICAL PROFILES
AND PREDICTED AREAS

- Arlington/College Hills (discussed on MSNBC)—three miles from Lee's girlfriend's apartment on Port Dr.
- Gourrier Avenue area (four miles from Lee's girlfriend's apartment on Port Dr.)
- West Lakeshore Drive area (without Kinamore's work location)— five miles from Lee's girlfriend's apartment on Port Dr.
- South Choctaw (using Kinamore's work location)—nine miles from Lee's girlfriend's apartment on Port Dr.
- South Twelfth Street, Port Allen (second anchor point)
- Renaud Drive, Scott, Louisiana (using only the Colomb crime locations)
- East of Highway 61 Emmett Bourgeois Lane—six miles from Lee's girlfriend's apartment on Port Dr.

KNOWN ADDRESSES ASSOCIATED
WITH DERRICK TODD LEE:

- 2533 Highway 10, Apt. 27, Jackson Place Apartments, Jackson, LA
- 4273 US 61, St. Francisville, West Feliciana Parish, LA
- 1717 Port Drive, Baton Rouge—girlfriend's apartment
- 12010 South Choctaw Drive, Baton Rouge—Ascension Ready Mix Concrete, Lee's employer from May to August 1999—four miles from Emmett Bourgeois Lane
- Plaquemine, Dow Chemical—Lee's place of employment until January 2002

Lee had a home in St. Francisville, Louisiana, about twenty-four miles north of Baton Rouge. St. Francisville was clearly not in my predicted area, and Baton Rouge police chief Pat Englade went on

TV criticizing my profile for being twenty miles off. And he was right. Like I said, Predator was twenty-four miles off. But why?

Because psycho-geographic profiling is more about science than hunch. Predator is only as good as the information available. Why, then, was Predator wrong? Because the Baton Rouge cops didn't link the Zachary murders to the Baton Rouge murders soon enough.

Neither did I.

After Lee's arrest, I carried out a reanalysis using the Warner and Mebruer crime locations in Zachary. Predator predicted the high-probability anchor point to be less than a mile from Lee's St. Francisville residence. I was still baffled. Why did Lee target and kill most of his victims in the southern part of Baton Rouge rather than going in other directions? Something just didn't add up.

Based on information contained in an affidavit for a search warrant again Derrick Lee, I discovered that he had a steady girl-friend named Sheila O'Neal, with whom he often stayed, for the better part of 2001 and 2002, at 1717 Port Drive in South Baton Rouge. Lee used his girlfriend's Port Drive address as an anchor point to travel out from, as demonstrated by the relatively minor distances traveled to the first three murders—Green's, Pace's, and Kinamore's—and to the fifth murder, that of Carrie Yoder. *(See map on page 135)*.

Lee was spending a lot of time within three miles of my pre-dicted anchor point. The Port Drive address shaped the mental map of Derrick Todd Lee. The distance between Baton Rouge and his St. Francisville residence provided Lee with a nice comfort zone.

Among the many mistakes that the task force made in inter-preting my profile was seeing my predicted area only as the possible location of the serial killer's place of residence, rather than as an alternate anchor point, in this case a place he frequently visited, namely his girlfriend's apartment. I had pointed out from the beginning that the predicted area could be the killer's home, parents' home, or girlfriend's residence.

Other mistakes of the Baton Rouge task force? After releasing numerous sketches of possible suspects, they failed to take seriously the sketch from the Pace murder, which showed the perpetrator to be African-American. Yet the task force chased a white man in a white truck. That was a major error.

The task force also relied on a DNA dragnet of at least twelve hundred men in Baton Rouge, which produced no results. In other words, they hoped that DNA from the crime scene could be matched to someone from their "phantom" list of twelve hundred suspects. That would require testing all twelve hundred for a match. I find this odd considering that, at this writing, a backlog of at least three hundred criminal cases awaiting DNA testing are collecting dust in the Baton Rouge evidence room while the perpetrators are left free to roam carrying out more violence.

The task force played no role in solving the serial murders. Most of the credit can be given to Zachary investigators and Danny Mixon, an investigator for the Louisiana State Attorney General's Office. Maybe Chief Pat Englade and Baton Rouge mayor Bobby Simpson should have hired Collette Dwyer.

After Lee's arrest, Good Samaritan Dwyer told reporters at a press conference that she had told the serial killer task force that she believed the serial killer was Derrick Lee. Dwyer said that she called and reported his suspicious behavior several times. The task force acknowledged that Dwyer phoned their tip line but said that cops told her that Lee did not fit the profile of a person of interest.

They ignored her tips, and yet, during a press conference on May 28, 2003, Baton Rouge mayor Simpson praised Chief Englade and the multi-agency serial murder task force. Simpson said, "This task force has been recognized as the best in the business, one of the most competent task forces that has ever been put together."

Derrick Todd Lee is currently on death row for the murder of Charlotte Pace.

CHAPTER **11**

STOLEN INNOCENCE: LITTLE LAURA SMITHER

THERE'S A FIFTY-MILE stretch of I-45 between Houston and Galveston, Texas, that I refer to as the Bermuda Triangle. It is the Dead Zone for missing and murdered women. In fact, so many women have gone missing or been found murdered along this stretch of road that one tabloid called the Gulf Freeway (I-45) "America's Highway to Hell."

In the last three decades, police from half a dozen states and at least two federal law enforcement agencies have chronicled at least thirty-two dead women in an area within a few miles of either side of I-45. The victims in the I-45 cases typically disappeared while out alone, only to be found dead and abused in a remote spot weeks or months later, leaving no clue as to their killer's identity or motive.

One of the first victims was Collette Wilson, age thirteen, who vanished from an Alvin, Texas, bus stop in 1971. When her body was found near Addicks Reservoir, police determined she had been shot in the head. About two weeks later, Brenda Jones, age fourteen, went missing. She disappeared while walking to Galveston Hospital to visit her aunt. Her body was found the next day, floating in Galveston Bay a short distance away. Jones had a slip stuffed in her mouth and had died of a gunshot to the head. Several months later, Allison Craven, age twelve, disappeared. She was seen leaving her apartmentt complex near I-45 South. Three months after that, some of Craven's body parts started turning up in a Pearland, Texas, field, about seven miles from where she was last seen. FBI agent Don K. Clark acknowledged in a newspaper interview in 2000 that there may be multiple serial killers responsible for the murders in the area.

In all, there have been about thirty-two murders of women and girls in Houston and the surrounding areas since 1971 which remain unsolved. Below is a list of females who have met their deadly fate along I-45. This is not an exhaustive list, but it does show just how deadly this section of I-45 really is.

LIST OF I-45 MISSING AND MURDERED VICTIMS

* **6/17/71, COLLETTE WILSON,** THIRTEEN, vanished from an Alvin bus stop; shot; body found near Addicks Reservoir.

* **7/1/71, BRENDA JONES,** FOURTEEN, vanished walking to a Galveston hospital; shot in the head; body found in the Galveston Bay area.

* **10/28/71, GLORIA GONZALES,** NINETEEN, shot in the head; body found thirty-five yards from Collette Wilson's body, near Addicks Reservoir.

* **11/9/71, ALLISON CRAVEN,** TWELVE, dismembered; body found in two locations, near her apartment in Harris County and in a Pearland field.

* **11/15/71, MARIA JOHNSON,** FIFTEEN, vanished from a Galveston shopping mall; shot in the head; body found at Turners Bayou, in Texas City.

* **11/15/71, DEBBIE ACKERMAN,** FIFTEEN, vanished from a Galveston shopping mall; shot in the head; body found at Turners Bayou, in Texas City.

* **01/03/73, KIMBERLY PITCHFORD,** SIXTEEN, disappeared from Pasadena, Texas, while driving to school; shot in the head; found in a ditch in the town of Angleton.

* **09/06/74, BROOKS BRACEWELL,** TWELVE, vanished from a convenience store pay-phone in Dickinson, Texas; beaten to death; body found in remote Alvin Swamp.

* **09/06/74, GEORGIA GEER,** FOURTEEN, vanished from a convenience store pay-phone in Dickinson; beaten to death; body found in remote Alvin Swamp.

* **11/1/80, FEMALE,** FOURTEEN TO SEVENTEEN, strangled with panty hose; found thrown to the side of I-45 north, five miles north of Huntsville.

* **1983, SANDRA RAMBERS,** body found near Friendswood.

* **08/31/83, SUSAN EADS,** TWENTY, raped and strangled; her nude body found in high grass near NASA Road 1 in Seabrook.

* **10/1/83, HEIDI (FYE) VILLAREAL,** TWENTY-THREE, disappeared from League City, Texas, convenience store payphone; beaten to death; body was found in the "dead zone" off Calder Road.

* **9/1/84, LAURA MILLER,** SIXTEEN, vanished from the exact same location as Heidi Fye; shot in the head; body was found in the "dead zone" off Calder Road.

* **AUGUST-DECEMBER 1985, JANE DOE 1,** approximately sixteen, missing from convenience store; shot in the back; body was found in the "dead zone" off Calder Road, along with the bodies of Fye and Miller.

* **10/07/88, RENE RICHERSON,** clerk from Galveston; vanished, still missing.

* **5/20/89, KIMBERLY NORWOOD,** last seen in Hallsville around 5:15 P.M. less than a mile from home; still missing.

* **10/08/91, JANE DOE 2,** body found in the "dead zone" off Calder Road; body was found in the same location as Fye, Miller, and Jane Doe 1.

* **01/05/92, KELLY DAE WILSON,** EIGHTEEN, last seen in the town of Gilmer.

* **04/16/92, MARIA ESTRADA,** TWENTY-ONE, disappeared from a bus stop near Houston; strangled; body was found a block from her home in a Dairy Queen drive-thru.

* **08/07/94, DIANA RoBOLLAR,** NINE, last seen walking to a Houston store; strangled; body was found in a vacant building close to where she disappeared.

* **07/06/95, DANA SANCHEZ,** SIXTEEN, vanished at a Houston phone booth; strangled; the I-45 killer called KPRC radio and revealed location of body, in a field near I-45.

* **02/01/96, LYNETTE BIBBS,** FOURTEEN, last seen at a Houston nightclub; shot in the head; body was found on a dirt road at the intersection of highways 10 east and 35 south.

* **02/02/96, TAMARA FISHER,** FIFTEEN, friends with Lynette Bibbs, last seen at a Houston nightclub; shot in the head; body was found with Lynette Bibbs's body on a dirt road at the intersection of Highways 10 east and 35 south.

* **03/05/96, KRYSTAL BAKER,** THIRTEEN, vanished from a Texas City convenience store; beaten, strangled, and sexually assaulted; body was found approximately twenty-five to thirty miles north of last seen location. Nearest highway from where last seen is I-45 S, and Highway 3 and 146.

* **04/03/97, LAURA SMITHER,** TWELVE, last seen jogging near her home in Friendswood, Texas; body was found in drainage ditch, partially dismembered. Key suspect, William Reece, is serving time for kidnapping.

* **06/07/97, ERICA ANN GARCIA,** FOURTEEN, last seen at a Houston teen nightclub; strangled; body found in vacant building near a hospital.

* **08/17/97, JESSICA CAIN,** SEVENTEEN, last seen by friends at Bennigans Restaurant off I-45 south at about 2:00 A.M. Her truck was found not far from the cut off to her home on I-45 S just north of Galveston Bridge; her body has never been found.

* **11/30/98, TINA FLOOD,** TWENTY-THREE, abducted from Webster nightclub parking lot; died in hospital on December 2, 1998.

* **12/08/98, MELISSA TROTTER,** NINETEEN, abducted from Montgomery College campus; body found January 2, 1999 in a wooded area fifty miles away.

Several suspects have been questioned about the I-45 murders. The strongest suspect is Dennis Patrick Lansbury, who was questioned about the string of murders in 2001. Lansbury, thirty-four, worked on the Calder Road property, near the "dead zone," where the bodies of four young women were found buried in the 1980s. Two of the four have never been identified. They are known simply as Jane and Jane Doe 2.

Lansbury became a suspect after he wrote a letter to the Fort Bend County sheriff, confessing to the murders of two Houston area women ten years earlier. Lansbury is currently serving 489 years in the Texas Department of Corrections for aggravated assault and an escape attempt. He has a lengthy criminal record.

After exhaustive interviews with Lansbury, in which he confessed to several other murders in the area, the Fort Bend sheriff and the FBI contacted League City Police, who promptly issued a bench warrant in order to interview him about the multiple homicides in the Calder Road area. Captain Chris Reed of the League City Police later said that "based on those interviews, Lansbury is considered a strong suspect in the League City murders." At the time of this writing Dennis Patrick Lansbury has not been charged in any of the I-45 murders.

Originally listed as one of the I-45 victims, Wanda May Pitts, age eighteen, vanished from a Shenandoah motel lobby on January 17, 1999. Some of her clothing, along with a skull later forensically matched to Pitts, was found in a heavily wooded area near the Montgomery-Walker County line. Once again, thoughts turned to the I-45 killer.

Things changed when Stuart Howard Stanton, thirty-eight, confessed to abducting and killing Pitts during a robbery. Stanton was an escaped mental patient from Colorado. He was sentenced to fifty years in prison for two unrelated attacks on women. His plea agreement stipulated that he could not be charged with the Pitts murder.

For a brief time in the spring of 1994, police investigators targeted Robert Don Weir, sixty-one, who owns the Calder Road property where four of the bodies were found. League City Police, working with the FBI, had concluded that one person was responsible for all four slayings. After a twelve-hour search of Weir's home, League City Police were later ordered to return his personal belongings when the FBI notified them that evidence sent for evaluation could not be linked to Weir. Weir would later say, "It's a great relief."

Laura Smither was the twelve-year-old daughter of Robert and Gay Smither of Friendswood, Texas. Everyone loved her. She had a way of bring joy to others—even strangers.

Smither could hardly wait to be a teenager. She was so excited that she had been counting down the days until her thirteenth birthday, according to her father Robert. The morning that she disappeared, she wrote on her message board, "Only 20 days 'til my birthday!"

Smither was a ballet dancer. She participated in the *The Nutcracker* every year, and was training at the Houston Ballet Academy. She was a Cadet Girl Scout working on her silver award, was a certified scuba diver, and loved the Houston Rockets basketball team. Smither had an extremely high IQ, and aspired to attend Stanford University.

April 3, 1997, was a quiet day like most mornings in her rural neighborhood. The sky was overcast. Although it was not routine for Smither to go jogging, she was getting in better shape for her ballet class. Prior to breakfast, she asked her parents' permission to go out for a short run. Smither took her Walkman and headphones but decided to put them in the mailbox when it started to sprinkle rain. She went out for her run and never returned home.

Bob and Gay Smither knew immediately that something was terribly wrong; their daughter always came home. Along with neighbors and family, the Smithers immediately began to search for her. Within the first hour of her disappearance, they filed a missing person report with the Friendswood Police Department. They distributed flyers with Smither's picture on it and used horses to search outlying areas.

By the end of the first search day, the news media began reporting on Smither's disappearance. By the start of the next search day, a battalion of Marines relocated their field exercises so that they could search for Smither while completing their operations. In all some 6,000 volunteers searched for her over seventeen days. Over one hundred detectives from surrounding police agencies came to assist the Friendswood Police Department, and the FBI assigned thirty agents to the case.

Seventeen days after Smither vanished, on April 20, the remains of a young female were found in a Pasadena retention pond fourteen miles from where she went missing. Following the autopsy on April 21, the medical examiner confirmed that the remains were Laura Smither's. Friendswood investigators noted some obvious similarities between her abduction and death and that of nine-year-old Amber Hagerman in Arlington three months earlier. Both girls' bodies were dumped in waterways, nude except for their socks.

I became involved in the hunt for Laura Smither's killer during the third year of my PhD studies at Liverpool University. My research into the crime scene actions of American serial killers had attracted the interest of criminal investigator Jay Lewis, then a detective for the Friendswood, Texas, police department and an investigator on the Laura Smither murder case.

Detective Lewis obtained my contact information from an online law enforcement discussion list and sent me an e-mail, asking if I would like to develop a psychological and geographical profile in the unsolved murder of Laura Smither. I promptly replied, indicating that I would agree to do the profiles provided that he could provide me case files on the murder. Detective Lewis mailed the case files to my home in Liverpool.

Normally, developing a valid geographical profile requires a series of crimes, usually three or more. The reason for this, as mentioned earlier, is that through the series, specific patterns should begin to emerge. However, in the Smither murder, I had only two locations with which to work.

The point of fatal encounter location is what I would have usually started with, but the exact site where Smither went missing was, at that time, unknown. Therefore, because she had not run far on that fatal morning, I used Smither's home address.

The second location that I used was the "dump site," that is, the retention pond in Pasadena where Laura's remains were found. The coordinates were fed into Predator, which responded with a "hit." Predator was showing a 53 percent probability that the offender lived in the vicinity of the South Houston area between South Houston and Humble Camp. The profiled area included the areas of East Haven, Genoa, and part of Skyscraper Shadows.

I-45 runs through this geographical area. Could Laura's death be more of the handiwork of the I-45 serial killer? I worked up the profiles and submitted them to Lewis on May 28, 1997.

PSYCHO-GEOGRAPHICAL PROFILE—LAURA SMITHER MURDER

My research on serial killers taught me that in child murders like Laura's case, where the victim was abducted close to home, it was highly unlikely that a drifter passing through the area had abducted and killed her. The reasoning behind this is based on extensive research that suggests that child killers who travel between cities and states killing dispose of their victims at considerable distances from where the victims go missing. This occurs because the victim's body carries the most evidential clues that could tie the offender to the murder.

This pattern usually includes distances between the abduction site and body dump site much greater than the distance between the crime locations in the Smither murder. Due to the nature of where Laura Smither was abducted and her body dump location, I felt that her killer was a local man. That didn't necessarily mean that it wasn't the I-45 killer operating close to home. But I was convinced whoever had killed Smither lived locally.

Another clue that pointed me to a local man was the time difference between the abduction date, April 3, and the date her body was found, April 20. I felt that since the ME's report suggested Smither had been in the water for five to six days, that still put her unaccounted for for at least a week. This, in addition to the proximity of the crime scenes, suggested to me that Smither may have been held captive during this timeframe in the local area.

My geographical profile in the Smither case provided two likely hypotheses:

1. THE OFFENDER ABDUCTED SMITHER AND LIVES IN THE AREA BETWEEN PEARLAND AND MOORE ROAD, AND THE BODY DUMPSITE WAS TO THWART THE POLICE INVESTIGATION. OR THE OFFENDER WORKS IN THE PASADENA AREA.

2. THE OFFENDER ABDUCTED SMITHER DURING A VISIT TO THE FRIENDSWOOD AREA DUE TO THE NATURE OF HIS WORK. HE THEN DISPOSED OF HER BODY EN ROUTE BACK TO HIS HOME BASE AREA.

As possible investigative steps that I offered to Friendswood investigators, I suggested that they obtain the zip codes for the areas that I had profiled the offender to live in, and then check those zip codes against police records for any individuals who may have had convictions involving children.

For my actual profile of the murderer, I started with the fact that over half of the child abduction murders in the United States are committed by a killer who is a stranger to the victim. Almost two-thirds of the killers had prior arrests for violent crimes, with more than half of the offenders having prior convictions for crimes against children.

A major weakness in previous child killer profiles was that there had been no attempts by profilers to differentiate between styles of child killers. Still today, there is no research published that scientifically establishes a categorization of child abduction-murderers that is directly relevant to police investigations. As a consequence, all child abduction-murderer profiles produced to date, by any group, have to be regarded as exploratory.

The process of classifying child abduction-murderers and their offenses is an intrinsically difficult and complex one; the data available are patchy, because the data were not originally collected for purposes of scientific analysis. I was able to overcome this weakness, at least in part, by looking more closely at what is called *offense dynamics*—how the "bad guy" acts before, during, and after the crime.

Through my research on 107 American serial killers and their interactions with victims, I've discovered that in selecting his victims, the killer prefers strangers, usually females, who are not targeted for any specific reason; any victim will do. The victim does not symbolize anyone or anything in particular to this killer. The symbolic category of likely victims is victims of opportunity. What might appear to represent targeting a specific victim type, a child, can often change in later murders to adults.

Characteristically, the offender will be averagely groomed and socially facile with others. These attributes will be reflected in his ease of obtaining victims. The approach often used is some form of a ruse, a ploy or con to draw the victim into his web. Once the victim is within his reach, he blitz attacks her. The action of this type of killer is characterized by a prolonged, bizarre, and ritualistic assault on his victims. The victim is nothing more to the offender than inanimate objects to be exploited. This type of killer gains psychological arousal by inflicting pain on his victims.

The killer makes contact with his victims in nondescript public places, for example, on the street, in a supermarket, nightclub, or public park. The killer's obsessions are his victims and how he can obtain them, whether they are children or other accessible targets, such as prostitutes. Whoever the victims are, bizarre sexual acts dominate the personal narratives of this killer.

The killer's behavior is classified as a cognitive-vehicle crime scene type. The killer shows power and control as can be seen in such acts as excessive mutilations. The experience of the act in itself excites and thrills him. The killer is a sadistic individual. He indulges himself with thoughts of bondage and sadism. He usually possesses a large stash of pornographic materials.

Sponsored by a plan of action, the offender will equip himself with a crime kit for torturing victims, for example, dismemberment tools. In these types of murders, the victim becomes a slave to the killer's distorted intimacy, which could result in the victim being retained for extensive periods of time prior to the murder. By the killer holding the victim captive, the offender is then free to terrorize the victim with extensive forms of bondage and domination scenarios.

Cognitive-vehicle killers usually bind and gag their victims using various devices, such as rope or handcuffs. The preferred methods of killing for this type of killer are ligature strangulation or stabbing. The victim's body will show signs of excessive stab wounds of ten or more, usually to the upper region of the body.

Restraints and weapons will be pre-selected and brought to the crime scene by the offender and removed from the crime scene. If an offender does not leave a restraint or weapon behind at the scene, that doesn't necessarily suggest the offender is forensically aware. Rather, the offender has rehearsed the murder over and over in his mind, which points to the fact the he has committed similar murders and will continue until arrested.

That's the point. When hunting a serial killer, police cannot get bogged down overanalyzing their forensics. Time is of the essence. The killer must be caught or he will continue to kill until he makes a mistake and is finally caught.

The victim's body will exhibit signs of methodical mutilation in the form of antemortem and postmortem cutting, slashing, and stabbing. The pattern of the cutting or hacking wounds will most likely reveal rough-edged, unskilled cutting rather than precise cutting wounds. Other signs of torture will include burns and small, short jabs with a pointed instrument, which is referred to as piqueuism.

Victims of a cognitive-vehicle killer will be disfigured postmortem, and their body parts buried, scattered, or submerged in water to prevent discovery. This behavior, that is, disfiguring, burying, and scattering body parts, reflects an offender who is forensically aware, who understands that leaving damaging evidence at the crime scene can link them to the murders.

The victim will show signs of antemortem sexual activity, most likely in the form of anal sex. Likewise, the victim will reveal signs of postmortem sexual activity as well, but evidence of semen is not likely to be found. Since the narrative of these men is to possess the victim's body, necrophilia is the preferred choice of sexual activity. Other evidence of sexual activity will include fellatio. Evidence of sexual exploration will be revealed in localized areas of the body in the form of skin tears or inserted objects.

Due to the offender's distorted search for intimacy with the victim after the murder, he will often retain souvenirs for psychological reflection. The souvenirs may be in the form of small, personal items or clothing of the victim. The souvenirs retained by the offender are usually hidden in a private chamber of horrors along with various devices for torture and murder.

For example, the locations may be the offender's basement, attic, or an outside storage building. Another way the offender retains memories of the hunts and kills is keeping a written diary and newspaper articles about the crimes. On rare occasions, the killer will relive his crimes by taking photos or videos of the victims before and after death.

The death site will not be the murder site. Often the victims' bodies are moved two or three times in an attempt to confuse the police, which leads to the mode of transportation being a late model vehicle, the kind that is not easily picked out. In an attempt to cover his tracks, the offender will hide the victims' bodies by such action as burying or burning, which, again, reflects forensic awareness.

On discovery, the victim's body will be posed, not staged. Staging is an attempt by the offender to cover their MO for the purpose of making the scene appear different. This is done to thwart the police investigation. Posing the victim's body can be for shock value when police first discover the body, or the posing may have some psychological meaning for the offender.

When the victim is found nude, her clothing will be hidden, found folded, or piled neatly near the body. This variable, clothing hidden, reflects forensic awareness, while finding the victim's clothing folded or piled neatly near the body carries psychological meaning for the offender and can be interpreted as a signature behavior. In some cases, the victim's clothing will be removed only from the waist-down. However, very little, if any, forensic evidence will be present at the crime scene of a cognitive-vehicle-type killer.

A cognitive-vehicle killer exhibits the uncanny ability to organize his lifestyle when non-offending, which allows him to segment his criminal interest into a private world of protected ritualism. Because of the offender's ability to appear conventional and law abiding, he can cunningly deceive others in his normal surroundings. This ability sees this type of offender's lifestyle separate from his criminal activities, which allows him to enjoy a social life. He may be divorced. His sexual orientation will be heterosexual rather than homosexual.

The offender's age range may vary. Although most cognitive-vehicle types commit their first murder by the age of thirty-five, it is possible that a late bloomer or undetected offender could bypass the central tendency of the age range. However, in the Smither murder, the offender's age is somewhere between twenty-eight and thirty-five years old. The offender's race will be white.

The offender's daily habits are often compulsive and structurally organized, which is reflected in how he carries out his murders. His work history may be tumultuous until he finds a position with minimum supervision. This type of offender often works or seeks to work in the semiskilled trades, such as factory positions, construction work, or auto repair. Educationally, he will be a high school graduate.

This type of offender will most likely have a violent criminal record. There may be misdemeanor convictions, for example, drunk driving or theft. If he has a military record, the records will reflect that his performance was good. The offender will not have a past record of mental, alcohol, or drug treatment. The use of chemicals or alcohol prior to the murders will not be a factor in crimes.

Now that the police had my profile, all I could do was wait.

Sometime in the early morning of May 17, 1997, Sandra Sapaugh, a topless dancer, pulled her van into a Stop-N-Go convenience store in Webster, Texas, to call a friend. While she was using the outside pay phone, she noticed a guy pouring water into the engine of a white pickup truck. She also noticed that the guy was staring at her intensely. After completing her phone call, she got in her van and headed to a nearby Waffle House restaurant to meet a friend.

After driving a short distance, Ms. Sapaugh heard a strange noise coming from her tire. She pulled into the parking lot of the Waffle House. Before she could get out of her van, the guy who had been staring at her appeared at her window. He explained that he noticed that she had a flat tire. Sapaugh got out of the van and saw that her tire was flat. The strange male offered to help.

The guy opened the hood of his truck and asked Sapaugh to reach into his truck and hand him a rag from the passenger side of the cab. As Sapaugh leaned into the truck, the stranger came up behind her, placed a knife to her neck, pushed her into the truck, and ordered her to stay down. He then drove to the parking lot of a Motel 6. He stopped the truck, reached into Sapaugh's shirt, and ordered her to remove her pants.

She refused. They left the motel parking lot. He drove North on Interstate-45 Sapaugh's legs on the stranger's lap. He again ordered her to remove her pants. She asked if she could take her shoes off first. He said she could, but to "hurry up." As she moved over to the passenger side and bent down, she opened the passenger door and prepared to jump from the moving vehicle.

When Sapaugh started to jump, the guy reached over and grabbed her shirt. But Sapaugh pulled free and jumped, hitting the ground, and rolling. Hearing his truck stop and start to back up, Sapaugh ran toward oncoming traffic. A passing motorist, Sandra Urekel, pulled over when she saw Sapaugh in the road. She pointed up the road to her attacker's pickup truck, which was now moving in reverse coming toward the women.

Urekel helped Sapaugh into her car and they drove back to the Waffle House to call the police. The Webster Police Department responded and an ambulance transported Sapaugh to an area hospital. William Lewis Reece, forty, was eventually arrested for the kidnapping of Sandra Sapaugh. Police also charged him with stealing bulldozers. Reece, a bulldozer operator, was living outside of Houston at the time of Laura's death.

In May 1998, he was found guilty of the kidnapping and sentenced to sixty years in prison in Huntsville, Texas. At the time of the Sapaugh kidnapping, Reece was on parole from Oklahoma for kidnapping, forcible oral sodomy, and rape. Police first suspected Reece of Smither's murder after learning that he had been working at a construction site off Moore Ranch Road. That is near where Smither was last seen jogging. On the morning she disappeared, Reece and other workers had been let go from work early because of rain.

Early in the Smither murder investigation, Reece had consented to a search of his truck, but police found no evidence tying him to Laura's disappearance. Also complicating the Smither investigation was that Laura's remains had been in the water too long to yield additional evidence. So, the cops had Reece for kidnapping, locked up for sixty years, but the Laura Smither case remains an open homicide.

The profiling information and investigative strategies that I offered to Detective Jay Lewis were totally ignored, even though the geographical profile turned out to be extremely accurate in predicting the general area where the prime suspect, William Reece, lived during the crime he was convicted of committing. On the map, the predicted search and home area is represented by a circle. Reece lived in a trailer, represented by a star, near the William P. Hobby municipal airport, which is just one mile from my predicted geographical area.

If Reece was indeed Smither's killer, several theories that I provided in my profile turned out to be accurate: he would have abducted Laura during a visit to the Friendswood area due to the nature of his work; he would have disposed of her body en route back to his home area.

If investigators had contacted me after I submitted the profiles, I would have suggested they use the zip code investigative method based on my geographical profile. This investigative strategy involves obtaining the zip codes for the area profiled. Using zip codes, investigators could have checked individuals against the Texas state criminal computer system who had previous sex convictions, were on parole, and lived in my predicted zone. The geographical profile in this case turned out to be very accurate despite the fact that my analysis included only two crime locations.

Not long after Laura Smither was murdered, on August 17, 1997, Jessica Cain, age seventeen, disappeared, last seen by friends at Bennigan's Restaurant off I-45 south at about 2 A.M. Her truck was found not far from her cutoff to home on I-45 just north of Galveston Bridge. Her body has never been found. If my geographical profile had been used to sniff out and investigative William Reece, Jessica Cain might be alive today.

William Reece has never been charged in the murder of Laura Smither despite evidence pointing to his guilt. One piece of evidence was a four-page letter sent to my attention in 2003 by a follow inmate of Reece's. In this letter the inmate claimed that Reece often talked at length about the murder of Laura Smither, even admitting to killing her.

There is certainly enough circumstantial evidence to charge Reece with the murder of Laura Smither. Police have fiber evidence that was collected from his truck that matches fibers found on Smither's socks. However, the District Attorney's office was leery of prosecuting the case, due to the length of time she had been in the water, the contaminants in the water, and the sad fact that Laura's autopsy was contaminated by the medical examiner's office.

A black hair from murder victim Rachel Crouch, whose autopsy was performed immediately prior to Smither's, was found on one of Smither's hands. The medical examiner refused to cite contamination in her report. Within a year she had been fired and filed a wrongful termination suit against the county. The ME won her suit, although she received no damages, only lost wages covering the time of termination to the time of the trial. No Texas medical examiner's office would hire her, and she eventually found work in a small town in Tennessee. She continues to claim that no contamination occurred in Smither's autopsy.

As for the Smither family, Bob and Gay Smither filed a wrongful death suit against William Lewis Reece in April 1999. Reece did not respond to the suit, and the Smithers received a default judgment against him, and damages of $110,000,000. For the Smithers, the money was not the reason for the law suit—after all, Reece is broke. As Dr. Bob Smither said, "I want him to know that we hold him accountable for Laura's death, even if the state has not charged him."

In my opinion William Reece is guilty of Laura Smither's murder. I based this conclusion on several factors. He has a violent criminal history of rape and kidnapping. He was working in the general area where Smither was jogging. Smither's body was found not too far from where Reece lived, and there was the letter that I received from Reece's fellow inmate in 2003. But it's my geographical profile analysis that Laura Smither's killer lived near my predicted area that ultimately convinces me of Reece's guilt.

CHAPTER **12**

DOUBLE MURDER AT PLISKIN RIVER

A PROFILE CAN BE based on many factors, and as a result, sometimes profiling can take a bizarre twist. Unexpected sources can shed new light on a case. The Pliskin, Idaho, 1996 double murder of the Andrews brothers has frustrated law enforcement for years. The boys were each shot three times in the head. One was severely beaten. The police have never solved the case.

Lt. Detective Paul Ryan of the Pliskin Police Department, who originally worked the Andrews murders, phoned me in 2003 and asked me to develop a profile in the case. Detective Ryan is trying to get the DA to review the case for possible charges.

In July 1996, the bodies of Frank and Kevin Andrews, ages sixteen and thirteen, were found in shallow water on the island portion of the Pliskin River. Frank's body was found first, by hikers, and Kevin's body was found the next day, about one hundred yards away.

Whenever a murder is committed, the first place detectives look for a suspect is the victim's next of kin. Seventy percent of homicides in this country are committed by people who know the victim. The classic motives for murder—jealousy, greed, hate, money—usually come from friends or relatives who have gotten into a dispute with the victim.

Detectives in the Andrews murders suspected that the surviving brother, Grady Andrews, might have had motive to kill. Investigation showed that he had had a rocky relationship with his siblings. But that didn't necessarily translate into murder, and there was no physical evidence tying him, or anyone else, to the crime.

Besides the case files Paul Ryan sent to me, which included forensics, the ME's report, crime scene photos, and the investigators' reports, he also included a copy of a poem Grady Andrews wrote for his brothers' funeral. The poem would subsequently be analyzed in a way that's a little different from how my high school English teacher taught me. But before I did that, police were asking for an immediate profile of the killer.

So I gave it to them.

PLISKIN, IDAHO DOUBLE HOMICIDE
Kevin Andrews # ME - C 71 99
Frank Andrews # ME - C 72 99

CRIME SCENE PROFILE

Homicide of KEVIN ANDREWS
- 13-year-old white male
- Investigated by Pliskin, Idaho Police Department and Wyatt County Sheriff's Office
- Medical Examiner's Office - Western Idaho Regional Medical Center
- M. E. Case # A 71 88

Homicide of FRANK ANDREWS

- **16-year-old white male**
- **Investigated by Pliskin, Idaho Police Department and Wyatt County Sheriff's Office**
- **Medical Examiner's Office - Western Idaho Regional Medical Center**
- **M. E. Case # A 72 88**

PSYCHOLOGICAL BEHAVIORAL PROFILE
OF CASE EVIDENCE, STATEMENT ANALYSIS
OF INTERVIEWS AND POEM

DR. MAURICE GODWIN - Ph.D.
Criminal Investigative Psychologist

FOR:
Lt. Detective PAUL RYAN
Pliskin Police Department

Note: *In a recent research study by Alison, Smith, and Morgan, the authors found that on examining 21 profiles developed by various individuals such as the FBI and criminologists, 24% of the predictions were ambiguous and 55% of the statements could not be verified if the offender was to eventually be arrested (such as the offender will have fantasized about the act in the weeks leading up to the offense). The study also found that 75% of the information contained in the 21 profiles was repetitious—meaning that it was information already known by police investigators.*

Based on the above study's findings, this report will not repeat the general case information already known by police investigators. When necessary the examiner will use case facts to support an assertion.

FOUNDATION FOR PROFILE REPORT
The following psychological and behavioral forensic profile was developed using available information supplied to the examiner by the Pliskin Police Department. The profile was developed from information such as crime scene reports, investigators' notes, crime scene photos, autopsy reports, witness statements, family interview transcripts, polygraphs of several family members and their examination transcripts, and written family records as referenced at the end of this report.

LOCATION
On Saturday July 16, 1996, Kevin Andrews, age 13, and his brother Frank Andrews, age 16, were murdered in Pliskin River Bottoms, in Pliskin, Idaho. This location by road is one mile from where the victims lived and roughly one-half mile by way of a short cut through the woods. The brothers were murdered on the Island portion of the Pliskin River Bottoms. Kevin Andrews's body was found on July 17, 1988 located approximately one-hundred yards to the east of where his brother, Frank Andrews's body was found on July 16, 1996 at 8:30 P.M. Both victims' bodies were located on the channel side of the Pliskin River. Two individuals walking in the river area found Frank's body.

ESTABLISHED TIMELINE OF VICTIMS AND EVENTS
The night before Kevin and Frank Andrews were murdered, they slept in a camper outside of their parent's residence. Sometime around

6:00 A.M. on July 16, 1988 the brothers woke up and got dressed to go to their irrigation pipe moving jobs for one of the local farmers. The modes of transportation that the brothers traveled to work on were two bicycles. Sometime between 10:00 A.M. and 10:30 A.M., Kevin and Frank finished their work. According to John Bocalela, who the brothers worked for, they received their paychecks. Bocalela stated that he saw the brothers riding their bikes while hanging on to co-worker Mac Peters's car.

Mr. Peters stated that Kevin and Frank rode their bikes beside his vehicle until they arrived home. In several interviews, Mr. Peters denied ever giving Kevin and Frank a ride to Pliskin; he finally changed his story during a Magistrate's inquiry and admitted that he did give the brothers a ride to town. Mr. Peters was cleared as a suspect in these murders. In the opinion of this examiner, there are discrepancies in the movement of the brothers after Mr. Peters dropped them off in Pliskin.

The only confirmed sighting of Kevin and Frank after they left their work was by Mr. Peters who last saw Kevin and Frank around 10:30 A.M. on July 16, 1988. In the opinion of this examiner, Mr. Peters either made a simple omission during his interview on July 18, 1988 with Officers Delguido and Delameter, purposely lied, or provided a key piece of evidence to solving these murders.

In Mr. Peters's interview with Officers Delguido and Delameter, the policemen stated that Grady Andrews, one of Frank and Kevin's brothers, arrived at the Falconcrest convenience store about 1:00 P.M. on July 16th in Milfine asking if he had seen Kevin and Frank and his response was "no." To be sure, Mr. Peters had seen the Andrews brothers earlier that morning around 10:30 A.M. when he dropped them off in Pliskin. It may be that Mr. Peters took Grady Andrews's question about seeing Kevin and Frank as meaning 'have you seen them recently?'

Considering that Mr. Peters's memory of that specific encounter with Grady Andrews was detailed—for example, he remembered speaking to Susie Andrews—it is therefore likely that he is being truthful. In the examiner's opinion, the encounter at the Falconcrest convenience store between Mr. Peters and Steve (victims' father), Susie (victims' mother), and Grady Andrews confirms that for some reason, these three family members were looking for Kevin and Frank.

After reviewing the statements made by neighbors to investigators about Kevin and Frank Andrews, they clearly show two kids that freely roamed their neighborhood, often causing mischief and problems that had brought the brothers to the attention of police. Neighbors also stated that they often heard arguing, screaming, yelling, and gunshot-like sounds coming from the Andrews's residence including the afternoon of the murders.

In the opinion of this examiner, it is unlikely that Steve and Susie Andrews would have become worried about the whereabouts of Kevin and Frank due to them being several hours late. Based on police interviews with Steve and Susie Andrews, Kevin and Frank arrived home at approximately 10:00 A.M. and two hours later (noon time) they started to worry and immediately went searching for them. In the examiner's opinion, based on all the available information, Steve and Susie's immediate concern for Kevin and Frank seems unlikely due to the brothers' past behavior.

The last known time that the brothers were seen alive was between 3:00 P.M. and 4:00 P.M. on July 16th. Andy Prine stated that the brothers cashed their checks at the Bronson convenience store. Prine's statement was supported by Gene Deising's statement. The latter said that he spoke to both Kevin and Frank Andrews by the coolers in Bronson's.

Where were Kevin and Frank during the 4 and a half hour time gap, 10:30 A.M. to 3:00 P.M., on July 16? There are no facts to establish their whereabouts during this time. In the opinion of this examiner, the brothers were at home. In the opinion of this examiner, some type of argument ensued between the two victims and Steve, Susie, and Grady, either individually or collectively. The two brothers then left their home around 1:00 P.M.

Based on police interviews with Grady Andrews's ex-wife, Leigh Francis, there was tension in the family, which centered on some form of past sexual abuse, that is, possible incest between Susie and her sons; Kevin and Frank had threatened to expose this abuse. The sexual abuse aspect will be discussed later in this report.

There are a lot of discrepancies in Steve, Susie and Grady's version of events surrounding the day of July 16, 1988. Susie Andrews originally told investigators that she went out to the camper Saturday morning to sleep after Kevin and Frank left for work. This is the same camper where Kevin and Frank had slept in Friday night July 15, 1988. Susie stated that she did not wake up until 11:00 A.M. Saturday morning. Steve stated that he first woke up about 7:45 A.M. Saturday morning and saw Grady Andrews standing in the bathroom washing up. Steve Andrews stated that he then went back to bed and he further stated that he was pretty sure that Grady did too.

However, Steve and Susie Andrews told detectives that the boys returned back home at approximately 10:00 A.M. How did Susie know the boys returned home at 10:00 A.M. Saturday morning if she did not wake up until 11:00 AM as she stated in her interview with detectives?

The Andrews' versions of events doesn't add up, especially when they originally stated that Kevin and Frank had changed out of their work clothes to clean clothes. The evidence suggests that Kevin and Frank had not changed their clothes. Steve stated he was awakened between 10:00 A.M. and 10:30 A.M. and Susie was supposedly awakened at 11:00 A.M. outside in the camper (although Steve states that she was cooking breakfast around 10:30 A.M.), and Grady had already been up.

In the opinion of this examiner, Steve, Susie or Grady would have likely heard Kevin and Frank return home, change clothes and leave again if these events actually occurred. In interviews with Steve, Susie and Grady, they gave the impression that Kevin and Frank left for work at 6:00 on July 16th and then completely disappeared after dropping off their bikes at home. In the opinion of this examiner, the statements of Steve, Susie, and Grady concerning the events of Saturday July 16, 1988 are at best contradictory, vexing, and misleading. In the opinion of the examiner, both Kevin and Frank arrived home after work to the full knowledge of Steve, Susie, and Grady. Kevin and Frank spent several hours at their home and possibly due to an argument left hurriedly. Steve, Susie, Grady and Brian (another brother) soon followed looking for them, which could account for Mr. Peter's run in with Grady Andrews around 1:00 P.M. at the convenience store, asking him if he had seen Kevin and Frank.

There is a discrepancy about who rode with Steve and Susie when they went looking for Kevin and Frank. Steve Andrews stated in his interview with investigators that Brian was left at home and Grady went with them. However, Peters stated in his interview that Brian was sitting in the back of the pick-up when he walked up to the truck after acknowledging Susie Andrews.

In the opinion of this examiner, Steve and Susie returned home and left Brian. Then Susie, Steve, and Grady went looking for Kevin and Frank alone. In the opinion of this examiner, one or possibly two individuals came across Kevin and Frank soon after they cashed their checks at Bronson's and gave them a ride. One witness stated that he passed a truck and saw Kevin and Frank in it with Grady driving.

The discrepancies in the timeline for Saturday July 16th between 10:30 A.M. when Mr. Peters dropped the brothers off in Pliskin and the last time they were witnessed alive suggest that Kevin and Frank knew their killer(s) and the murders were not committed by strangers. In the opinion of this examiner, Steve, Susie, and Grady were not being completely honest with police investigators during their initial and follow-up interviews about the events surrounding the movements of Kevin and Frank on Saturday July 16, 1988 after the brothers returned home from work.

INVESTIGATIVE RECOMMENDATIONS

It is the suggestion of the examiner that the timeline discrepancies should be thoroughly explored in any future interviews with the Andrews family members. Direct questions should be asked in order to pin the interviewee down to specific times, to see if the interviewee will change his/her story reflecting further discrepancies.

In the opinion of the examiner, the Andrews family members were not being completely truthful during their interviews. For example, a statement analysis of Grady Andrews's interview dated October 19, 1988 with the Pliskin investigator indicates that Grady Andrews was being evasive and selective in what he could and could not remember. Grady Andrews's evasive and deceptive responses (shown in italics below) indicate that he was not being honest with the investigator and suggests that he had something to hide.

The statements below of Grady Andrews are verbatim and taken from the October 19th interview:

"Okay, I can remember, let me see, it was Friday, **I can't remember** if they did the pipe, considering it was Friday they must have went to school.

"Oh, that's right there was no school, jeez, okay. So they went and moved the pipe. **I can't remember** that day but I can remember my mom was pickling or something.

"Okay, she was doing canning or something, **I can't remember** what she was canning, but she was canning. Beets, she was canning beets, anyway that night I—I was gone all night.

"**I don't remember.** It's been off here and there every so often. Yeah, we were going, well, first there was Frank and Bryan, just put a mattress out there and we were going to sleep outside. And I didn't want to and they go come on sleep outside with us and I ended up sleeping out there.

"No, I got up in the morning, about six, got up, went and took a bath and went back and hit the sack again about seven cause I was real tried.
"Uh-hun, sometime around there. **I don't remember** anyway I know it

was an hour I was up, sometime around six, but I know it wasn't—And I did see Frank still asleep when I got up. I know I gave the correct time last time."

Mr. Andrews's use of the pronoun "they" during his interview to reference his deceased brothers reflects a lack of empathy and conscience. Grady Andrews spoke of his brothers as though they were objects. Grady Andrews's entire interview was replete with similar impersonal nouns and the inability to remember simple details.

AUTOPSY REPORT
TIME OF DEATH ESTIMATES
The autopsy report did not specify a time of death for either victim. An examination of the crime scene and autopsy photos show that post-mortem lividity (the red discoloration in the skin caused by the pooling and settling of the blood within the blood vessels) was present in Kevin Andrews's body. Lividity begins about thirty minutes after death. It takes about 8 to 10 hours for lividity to become fixed. However it is only one biological indicator, and no one indicator alone should be used to determine the time of death.

Rigor Mortis (the chemical process of the exhaustion of ATP in muscle tissue, which begins after death that results in the stiffening or contracting of muscles in the body) was present in Kevin Andrews as evident in the crime scene and autopsy photos. This finding is expected because Kevin's body was found a day after the murders.

As a general biological guideline, Rigor Mortis begins about 2 to 4 hours after death. Full Rigor Mortis is complete about 8 to 12 hours after death. Cold slows Rigor Mortis down, and heat speeds the process up, which means that the water would have slowed down the

Rigor Mortis. By itself, the use of Rigor Mortis to determine a time of death, or a time range of death, is not advised. Several biological indicators and other factors should be used as discussed below.

Based on eyewitnesses who last saw Kevin and Frank between 3:00 PM and 4:00 P.M. and the recording of gun like sounds by an individual at a family reunion near the crime scenes, in the examiner's opinion the time of death was between 5:00 P.M. and 8:30 P.M. Saturday July 16, 1988.

The timelines provided were produced from interview transcripts of the victims' family, friends, neighbors, and others. This is not a time line that was put together by Pliskin Police or any other agency. Also, times of deaths are supported based on the time it takes skin to wrinkle while exposed to water.

KEVIN ANDREWS

CLOTHING
The victim was wearing blue-gray extremes shirt, blue jeans, socks with blue and white stripes, white, blue, and black high-top shoes. Victim also possessed a small amount of change in his pockets and a small watch with no band.

WOUND PATTERN ANALYSIS
Gunshot wound one was to the base of the neck with bullet passing through the soft tissue of the neck stopping near the right mandible, which is the largest and strongest bone of the face. Gunshot wound two was to the left occipital pole with the bullet passing through the left side of the brain and recovered from the left gyrus. Gunshot wound three was to the right skeletal area with the bullet passing

through the right frontal lobe and recovered from the right side of sella turcia. Sella turcia is a bony saddle-like structure above the sinuses at the back of the nose.

In this examiner's opinion, two gunshots were fired at close range, probably one foot or less. This opinion is based on a review of autopsy photos of the gunshot entrance wounds that showed considerable tattooing caused by imbedded gun powder particles and dense smoke deposits. One shot was fired at a distance of 5 feet or more. The shot fired at a distance was determined based on the location of one wound on top of the head and the fact that there was no smoke halo, limited tattooing, and no singeing of bullet hole-edge.

In the opinion of this examiner, Kevin Andrews was shot twice, execution style (kneeling position). This style of killing indicates a calculated murder with the double-tap procedure. Double- tap is a reference to the quick, successive, and coordinated shots that form a close shot pattern or group. A double-tap indicates calculation not recklessness. The main reason for a double-tap after the first shot was to ensure that the victim would die. The double-tap method of murder could have been done without actually knowing the procedure or the method could have been learned by reading gun or survivalist magazines.

The victim had a 'Y' shaped laceration on the top of his head with the laceration to the right of the head looking from behind. The 'Y' shaped laceration revealed crushing of the skull from several directions. There was evidence that victim was hit numerous times in both eyes, which was likely received during a fistfight. Victim also had linear abrasions on the left side of his back. These abrasions could be from drag marks; however, it is most likely they occurred from being pushed down the riverbank, the victim's back brushing against tree limbs and brushes as he fell. The victim's shirt on his left side was pulled up around his neckline, which exposed this portion of his back. This could indicate that the victim was either dragged by his shirt from the left side or dragged by his feet to the riverbank.

In the examiner's opinion, the victim was initially struck on the head in order to incapacitate him. In the examiner's opinion, Kevin Andrews, not Frank Andrews, was the focus of the entire attack and murder. This is evident due to the massive blunt trauma to the victim's head. The attack to victim Kevin Andrew's head went beyond what was needed to render the victim dead. In other words, the three gunshots alone were enough to kill the victim; the severe beating to his head went beyond the need to murder the victim—**it was personal.**

In this examiner's opinion, blunt force to the victim's head is a signature behavior. Signature behavior is comprised of the actions committed by the offender that are not necessary for the completion of the crime; behavior that the offender did not have to do. Signature behavior is different from an offender's **modus operandi** (MO). The offender's MO is comprised of the actions that are necessary for the completion of the crime.

The attack to Kevin Andrews's head suggests hatred and rage towards the victim. The perpetrator used extreme force to Kevin's head, using some type of blunt object. The object marks may be consistent with a crowbar or pry bar, which could indicate that the perpetrator used a vehicle to travel to the crime scene and was not on foot. It is unlikely that the butt of a gun or rock caused the injuries considering the linear shape of the wounds.

SEXUAL ASSAULT/ RAPE INDICATORS

Based on a review of all documents in this case, Kevin Andrews suffered no sexual assault.

DEFENSE INJURIES

Kevin Andrews's body showed no sign of being restrained. This could indicate that he went willingly to the location where he was killed, which suggests that he most likely knew his attacker. Kevin Andrews suffered defense injuries to his eyes and inner lip. In the opinion of the examiner, the victim received these injuries during a fistfight. These injuries could have occurred before the victim was taken to Pliskin River Bottoms. In the opinion of the examiner it is unlikely that a fistfight ensued at the murder location, considering that the perpetrator(s) were armed. The victim was controlled at this point with a gun and most likely offered minimum resistance out of fear. In the opinion of the examiner, there is an unknown primary crime scene where the victim was initially assaulted.

FRANK ANDREWS

CLOTHING

The victim was found wearing white cut-off T-shirt, white cotton briefs, and Wrangler blue jeans—36-30. Victim possessed a small amount of change in his pockets. The victim's shoes were Nike Court tennis shoes, blue in color with no socks. Victim's wet socks were found on the riverbank.

WOUND PATTERN ANALYSIS

Frank Andrews suffered three gunshot wounds to the head. Gunshot one entered near the right ear and was recovered in the right temporal bone. Gunshot two entered the right temporal area and was recovered in the left temporal lobe. Gunshot two caused severe injury to the mid-brain section. Gun shot three entered the right occipital and was recovered in the left temporal muscle.

In the examiner's opinion, two gunshots were fired at medium range, probably three to five feet. This opinion is based on a review of autopsy photos of the gunshot entrance wounds that showed some tattooing and some singeing at the edge of the bullet holes. One shot was fired at a distance of five feet or more. The shot fired at a distance was determined based on the location of one wound on top of the head and the fact that there was no smoke halo, limited tattooing, and no singeing of bullet hole-edge.

In the opinion of the examiner, Frank Andrews was shot twice while kneeling or bent over. Like Kevin, the double-tap procedure was also used on Frank in at least two of the shots. If all three shots were fired at the same time, it is most likely that the shots would have been in the same area of the head. As previously stated, this style of killing indicates a calculated murder with the double-tap procedure.

In addition to the three gunshots, the victim had four lacerations to the left eye with evidence of tissue hemorrhaging. The victim also had superficial linear abrasions on the left side of his back, in a similar location to abrasions found on Kevin Andrews's back.

SEXUAL ASSAULT/ RAPE INDICATORS

Based on a review of all documents in this case, Kevin Andrews suffered no sexual assault.

DEFENSE INJURIES

Frank Andrews's body showed no sign of being restrained. This could indicate that he went willingly to the location where he was killed. This suggests that it was likely that Frank knew his attacker. Frank Andrews suffered defense injuries (lacerations) to his left eye. In the opinion of the examiner, the victim received these injuries during a fistfight. These injuries could have occurred before the victim was taken to Pliskin River Bottoms. In the opinion of this examiner, is unlikely that a fistfight ensued at the murder location considering that the perpetrator(s) were armed. The victim was controlled at this point with a gun and most likely offered minimum resistance out of fear. In the opinion of the examiner there is an unknown primary crime scene, which would be the same unknown primary crime scene associated with Kevin Andrews's assault.

INVESTIGATIVE RECOMMENDATIONS

It is recommended by this examiner that a forensic pathologist be consulted to examine the impressions that made the depressed skull fractures to Kevin's head. The purpose of this expertise would be to ascertain, with a degree of scientific certainty, what type of instrument likely caused the blunt trauma to the head. Having this kind of investigative information, new leads could be developed.

Both murders appeared to be committed with twenty-two-caliber ammunition. Evidence found at the crime scenes by Pliskin detectives suggests that the bullets were .22 Winchester Super X brand. Relying on the documents provided to this examiner, I was unable to ascertain with any certainty if the weapon was a handgun or rifle. However, considering the Super X brand of ammunition and the fact that at least several shots were fired at a distance, it is likely that a rifle was used.

In the opinion of the examiner, it may be helpful to consult a firearms expert. For example, .22 bullets can be fired from a .308 rifle using 22/30 Sabot ammunition. This could mislead investigators. The shooter(s) could have altered or removed the shell casings from the crime scene, hindering the true identification of the type of weapon used. This is especially true of the local area where the victims were found, because this location is known to be a place where people often do target practice.

The autopsy revealed that .22 bullets were used but a .308 rifle could have been used or both. Several .308 shell casings were found at Frank Andrews's crime scene. Knowing what type of weapon that was used in a murder could later assist investigators in properly identifying similar weapons and ammunition during the search of a suspect's home. In the opinion of this examiner, a 22/30 sabot may have been used during the commission of these murders.

In the opinion of the examiner there is an unknown primary crime scene, indoors, where the victims were initially assaulted.

VICTIMOLOGY AND RISK ASSESSMENT
KEVIN ANDREWS
FRANK ANDREWS

The information available to this examiner regarding these victims was based on police interviews with ex-family members and the Andrews' neighbors.

In the opinion of this examiner, Kevin and Frank lived day-to-day in a dysfunctional family situation. The same was true for all of the Andrews children. Kevin and Frank worked part-time jobs but they had to share their minimum earnings with their parents to pay bills. The brothers basically had no parental supervision, although their parents Steve and Susie Andrews tried to give the impression in interviews with investigators that they were strict and caring parents.

In the examiner's opinion, the parents had no supervision over Kevin and Frank. Kevin and Frank often roamed their neighborhood and on several occasions carried out acts of vandalism and thefts, which caused problems with local neighbors. In the examiner's opinion, both Kevin and Frank were defiant children with tendencies towards destructive, anti-social behavior.

Kevin and Frank were friends with several local boys possibly involved in drugs, which put them at low to medium risk. However, in the examiner's opinion, is unlikely that these relationships led to their deaths. Police investigators investigated and cleared these acquaintances, including any neighbors, of being involved in their deaths.

In the examiner's opinion, the potential for high risk of violence likely came from within the Andrews's home. An examination of interview transcripts of Grady Andrews's ex-wife, Leigh Francis, provided this foundation, suggesting that Kevin and Frank were being sexually abused by their brother Grady and possibly by their own mother Susie Andrews.

Statements made by Ms. Francis to investigators indicated that Susie often compared the penis sizes of her sons. In the opinion of the examiner, Susie Andrews's incestuous acts contributed to the build up of tension, anger, and jealously between her sons.

This coupled with incestuous acts possibly carried out by Grady on his brothers, paved the way in creating an environment and situation that placed Kevin and Frank at high risk for harm.

In the opinion of this examiner, Grady and Susie Andrews felt that they were losing control over Frank and Kevin. Grady and Susie Andrews feared they could not control Kevin and Frank from revealing to others and the police a history of sexual molestation. In the examiner's opinion, it was this fear that set the stage for the murders.

CRIME SCENE CHARACTERISTICS
CRIME SCENES
Generally, there are two types of crime scenes: primary and secondary. A primary crime scene is most often defined as the scene where the most interactions between the victim and the offender take place. All other locations associated with a crime are defined as secondary crime scenes.

KEVIN ANDREWS
Kevin Andrews's body was found on the Southside of the river.

Considering there were two victims, normally there would be only two primary crime scenes. However, in Kevin's murder, there is one known primary crime scene and one unknown primary crime scene, as previously mentioned. The examiner will call the known primary crime scene (A), which is the mound where blood spatters on the rocks, blood on the ground, and the victim's hair were found.

CRIME SCENE LABELS – KEVIN ANDREWS

A – Rocks with blood – **Primary**
B – Unknown Scene – **Primary**

SECONDARY CRIME SCENES

C – .22 shell casings were found
D – One rock with blood was found
E – Riverbank location
F – Location where body was found

At primary scene **(A)**, evidence suggests that the victim was dragged across the rocks and leaves towards the riverbank. In the opinion of the examiner, it is odd that no evidence of blood drippings between primary scene **(A)** and the riverbank were found. What could account for this lack of blood could be the position the victim was dragged. Primary crime scene **(A)** is the most likely area where Kevin was shot and bludgeoned to death. There is no documentation of blood being found at the location where the shell casings were found.

The second primary crime scene **(B)** is unknown. In the opinion of the examiner, Kevin Andrews received his facial defense wounds at another location away from the Pliskin River Bottoms and then was escorted to the river at gunpoint. If investigators can determine the location of primary crime scene **(B)**, then these murders could possibly be solved.

There are at least four secondary crime scenes associated with Kevin Andrews's murder. The examiner will call these secondary scenes

(C), (D), (E), and (F). *Secondary scene* (C) *is where the .22 shell casings were found. Primary crime scene* (A) *is roughly 47 feet from secondary crime scene* (C). *In the examiner's opinion, either the offender(s) fired a shot from this location, or threw the shell casings over into this area. No blood was found at secondary scene* (C).

Secondary scene (D) *is the location where one rock was found that had the victim's blood and hair on it. The rock could have been tossed in to this area. Secondary scene* (E) *is the location at the riverbank tree where blood and hair evidence from Kevin Andrews was found by investigators suggesting that at some point the victim's head was placed against the bark of the tree leaving forensic evidence. Forensic evidence of blood was also found on leaves next to the tree. No shell casings were found at this scene.*

Secondary scene (E) *is by the edge of the water, approximately nine feet down an embankment. The distance from secondary crime scene* (E) *to scene* (C) *is between 81 to 85 feet. Secondary crime scene* (F) *is the location where Kevin Andrews's body was found in the river. Secondary scene* (F) *is approximately 39 feet from primary crime scene* (A).

FRANK ANDREWS

There are two primary crime scenes associated with Frank Andrews's murder. His primary crime scene one will be referred to as (AA).

At primary scene (AA), *investigators found a pool of blood. Primary scene* (AA) *is located approximately 100 yards from primary scene* (A), *Kevin Andrews's primary scene. The distance from the pool of blood (primary scene AA) to secondary scene C—the location of shell casings at Kevin's murder scene—is approximately 318 feet.*

The second primary crime scene referred to as **(BB)** is unknown. In the opinion of the examiner, Frank Andrews received his facial defense wounds at another location away from the Pliskin River Bottoms and was then escorted to the river. If investigators can determine where primary crime scene **(BB)** is, then these murders could possibly be solved.

CRIME SCENE LABELS – FRANK ANDREWS

AA – Blood pool – Primary
BB – Unknown Scene – Primary

SECONDARY CRIME SCENES

CC – .22 & .308 shell casings found
DD – Location where body was found
EE – Riverbank where socks were found
FF – Shoe prints & Boot print on riverbank

There are four secondary crime scenes associated with Frank's murder. The first secondary scene is referred to as **(CC)**. This location is where the .22 and .308 shell casings were found. The distance from primary scene **(AA)** to secondary scene **(CC)** is 9 feet. The second secondary crime scene is referred to as **(DD)**. This location is where the victim's body was found in the river. Evidence found suggested that Frank Andrews's body was dragged from the primary crime scene **(AA)** to the edge of the riverbank. The third secondary crime scene **(EE)** is the location on the riverbank where Frank's wet socks were found. One sock appeared to be stretched considerably, which could indicate that it was removed with force.

The fourth secondary crime scene **(FF)** is the location on the riverbank where Frank's and Kevin's shoeprints were found. This examiner *examined and confirmed that the two known shoeprints matched the shoes that Kevin and Frank were wearing. Based on this evidence, in the opinion of this examiner, both victims were initially taken to secondary crime scene* **(FF)**.

At the very least, this finding indicates that Frank and Kevin were together while standing at secondary crime scene **(FF)**. *Another photo not shown in this report of Frank's bare footprint suggests that his shoes were removed at this same location. This location is in the same general area as the photo above.*

In the examiner's opinion, Kevin either tried to escape and was caught or was escorted down the rock path at gunpoint to primary crime scene **(A)**. *To the right of the two known shoeprints is a partial boot print that has not been identified. The boot print could have been possibly made by one of the investigators; however, in the opinion of the examiner, the boot print should be examined further.*

In the opinion of this examiner, this crime as it stands is at least one crime scene short of being solved. That is to say that there are at least three primary crime scenes associated with the two murders: (1) Kevin's murder location; (2) Frank's murder location; (3) the unknown primary location where both victims engaged in a fistfight with their killer(s).

METHOD OF APPROACH

The victims were last seen together cashing their checks. There is no documentation to say that a witness saw the brothers leaving the Bronson convenience store parking lot. Frank Andrews kept his money hidden in his sock, which was only known to family members. Frank's socks were found laying on the riverbank and only a small amount of change was found in his pockets. These elements together suggest that someone knew the victims and that the victims trusted their killer(s). In the opinion of this examiner, the victims were initially assaulted in one location and forced at gunpoint to travel to the river. The lack of any restraints could support this.

Since it is common for family members who live together to have easy access to each other, the method of approach in this case was not a con or ploy but rather started out as an argument, turned into a fight, then turned to a violent blitz attack to gain control, which ultimately involved the use of a firearm. In the opinion of the examiner, it may be important to consider that neighbors of the Andrews heard yelling coming from their house on the afternoon of the murders.

METHODS OF CONTROL

The assailant(s) in this case controlled their assault on these two victims with very specific, deliberate methods. The toxicology report showed no signs of alcohol or drugs in the victims, so they were fully aware of what was happening.

Firstly, the victims were initially attacked in a secure location such as a house in order to avoid attracting attention and for controlling any possible noise.

Secondly, the assailant(s) delivered blows to the victims' facial areas, which were corrective in nature, that is to say, delivered with the intent to gain compliance. However, it is clear that the main head injuries to Kevin Andrews were rageful in nature, being deep, forceful, and resulting in extensive skull damage.

Thirdly, the assailant(s) removed the victims to a location that the assailants were familiar with, where they could feel dominant and establish their authority without being discovered or heard. The landscape along the trail to where the victims were murdered is narrow and secluded by thick trees and bushes on both sides. This location provided a perfect backdrop for the murders. The location was also convenient to the Andrews's house. The river is approximately 1 mile by car and a half mile by foot through a path in the woods from the Andrews's house.

AMOUNT OF FORCE

There was a high level of suddenly applied physical force used to gain these victims' initial compliance before they had been removed to primary crime scene **(AA)**.

Kevin Andrews received the highest level of brutal physical force. As previously mentioned, in the examiner's opinion, this entire crime was directed towards Kevin Andrews. Kevin's murder was overkill. Overkill is defined as excessive trauma or injury, beyond that necessary to cause death.

Although these murders were deliberate as evidenced by the double-tap procedure in shooting the victims, the violence also indicates an extremely reactive, angry, retaliatory offender. Kevin and Frank Andrews were being punished for some real or perceived wrongs. Their killer(s) would have not bargained with or listened to the victims' pleas. From their point of view, the killer(s) were only concerned with teaching the victims a lesson.

VICTIM RESISTANCE

The victims offered only limited resistance to these attacks. This is demonstrated by the limited amount of defensive injuries noted in the autopsy report. This speaks to the sudden, unexpected blitz attack from, in the examiner's opinion, two offenders. It also suggests that soon after the initial assaults, a firearm was used to gain control over the victims.

FORENSICALLY AWARE ACTS

Precautionary acts are behaviors that the offenders purposefully engage in to protect their own identities, facilitate their escape from the scene, and destroy or deny the transfer of physical evidence. A simple example would be a rapist who wears a mask and uses a condom; both are forensic precautionary acts. This case has several forensic precautionary acts that were used by the offenders.

The following are examples of forensic precautionary acts carried out by the offenders. The examples are not meant to be all-inclusive list, but rather to demonstrate the offenders' state of mind before, during and after the murders:

1. Removal of the victims to an isolated location known to the offenders that the offenders controlled. This provided the killers with the time to engage in those activities that they desired.

2. Disposal of the bodies in water: This act very effectively washes all of the physical transfer evidence from the bodies of the victims. Disposing victims in water is also an attempt to place the victims at a location separate from the killers.

NUMBER OF ASSAILANTS

It is the opinion of this examiner that there were two perpetrators in this case. In the opinion of this examiner, a male was responsible for *the beatings and murders but was assisted by an older accomplice. The crime scene presentation is more consistent with two killers than with one. This is for the following reasons:*

1. The number of victims assaulted and killed would have been more easily accomplished with two perpetrators.

2. It would have been easier to inflict the range of injuries on Kevin Andrews with two perpetrators, especially considering that control over Frank Andrews during the attack had to be maintained. Even if we considered that Frank was murdered first, his crime scene location was 100 yards from Kevin's crime scene; a second perpetrator had to maintain control over Kevin Andrews.

3. Given that the size of the entire crime scene area is roughly 90 feet in width and 100 yards in length, one perpetrator would have a difficult time controlling the victims; two perpetrators would have more ease.

OFFENDER PERSONALITY CHARACTERISTICS

There are very likely two offenders involved in the deaths of Kevin and Frank Andrews. This profile section will focus on the background characteristics of the primary killer, the individual who actually beat and shot the victims. Since the murder case is 16 years old, this profile will focus on the characteristics of the killer at the time the murders occurred, which was in 1988. The second offender in these murders assisted in covering up the crime, destroying forensic clues and helped maintain control over the victims.

Robbery was not the motive for the murders. Drugs were not the

*motive for the murders. The primary killer committed these murders
due to issues involving jealousy, possessiveness, and ultimately
fear of being found out about sexual abuse related issues. He wanted
to punish the victims and to re-establish sexual ownership of
another person, most likely an Andrews family member. He may
have engaged in prior homosexual and heterosexual relationships.*

*He is superficial, but also extremely venerable to manipulation. He is
easily controlled. He has an explosive personality, one who is impulsive, quick-tempered. He is reclusive and has trouble fitting into the
crowd. He is incapable of accepting responsibility for his own
actions. He blames everyone else.*

*He is the type of individual who keeps written documentation of his
thoughts similar to a diary. This is his way of reliving the events. The
documents will likely to be in the form of poems, songs, or just narratives. The syntax will be poor and illogical. Paragraphs will appear to be
rambling and on first examination will not make much sense. He will
keep these documents hidden in a 'secret' place that might be pad
locked or hidden in a closet, attic, wall, or underneath floorboards.
Computer hard drives, floppy disks, and CDs should be examined. He
is aware that the nature of these written documents could implicate
him in the murders, which is why he keeps the materials hidden. He is
the type of individual who would retain these materials years after the
murders. He is the type of individual who would write new narratives
related to these murders. As such, investigators should look for these
documents during a search of the suspect's residence.*

ARREST HISTORY
*He does not have a criminal record. The individual who assisted him
may have minor violations. While neither offender has a criminal*

record of violence, in the opinion of this examiner, both individuals covered up the crime and/or discussed ways to destroy forensic evidence.

MARITAL STATUS

He was not married at the time of the murders.

RESIDENCE

He lives within a few miles of the crime scenes. It is very likely, in fact, that he was part of the search effort for Kevin and Frank, and that he placed the bodies in a specific location with perhaps the intent of being the one to later find them in an attempt to shift the blame. This may account for the log being placed across Kevin's neck.

SKILL LEVEL

Given the geographical location of these murders, and the fact that the offender was likely a local resident with a great familiarity with the area and the habits of the people in the area, it is not likely that the offender is educated past the high-school level. He would have performed poorly in school due to his aggressive nature, intolerance for others, and his overall impatience.

In the opinion of this examiner, both perpetrators demonstrated a wealth of forensic knowledge. However, in the opinion of this examiner, the killer was instructed by his accomplice not to leave obvious physical evidence behind at a crime scene without making some attempt to obscure it.

EMPLOYMENT

It is very unlikely that he was employed. He lacks the skills, discipline, and patience to hold down a full-time job.

TRANSPORTATION

It is very unlikely that he owned a vehicle. His accomplice may have owned an older-type vehicle.

AGE

He was 18 to 20 years old.

MILITARY SERVICE

He had no military service at the time of the murders.

INVESTIGATIVE CONSIDERATIONS

Based on the discrepancies in Steve, Grady, and Susie Andrews's version of events on the day of the murders, in the opinion of this examiner Kevin and Frank Andrews were murdered by at least two individuals who had intimate knowledge of the Pliskin River Bottoms. In the opinion of the examiner, the two offenders had intimate knowledge of Kevin and Frank's Saturday schedule and whereabouts. In the opinion of this examiner, the killers had knowledge of the money that Frank kept in his socks. Removal of the socks and possibly the money was to give the appearance of robbery.

Investigative consideration should be given to the below information, which was taken from Grady and Susie Andrews's interview transcripts and Grady Andrews's ex-wife's interview transcript.

This examiner finds it highly suspicious that Grady Andrews had a fairly detailed memory of the day of the murders but can't remember the day before was still summer and that there was no school.

[Grady's timeline reference] Grady recalls the time he was up on Saturday morning after sleeping in the trailer ". . . . Was sometime

around there [6:00 A.M.]. I don't remember anyway, I know it was an hour I was up, sometime around six . . ." and "I did still see Frank asleep when I got up. I know I gave the correct time last time."

The above statement indicates deception. Rather than come up with another time, or try to remember his original story, he cops out with "I know I gave the correct time last time."

Grady's statements indicate that he has a deceptive personality, which means that he is capable of hiding forensic evidence.

[Susie's timeline reference] ". . . .get(s) them up, I always get them up."

What is suspicious about Susie Andrews's version of events that Saturday morning is that she claims to have got Kevin and Frank up from the camper that they were sleeping in yet insists that she went to the camper and fell asleep and did not wake up until 11:00 A.M.? However, Grady stated that "he woke up from hearing his mother talking. Grady says "See mom was talking or something and I woke up, I usually wake up around 10:00 A.M.."

Steve stated in his interview that "he was up between 10:00 A.M. and 10:30 and had Brian call to Grady to wake him up and come eat breakfast." Steve stated that, "Susie was cooking."

How could Susie be up cooking breakfast between 10:00 A.M. and 10:30 while she was still be asleep in the camper trailer until 11:00 A.M.?

In the examiner's opinion, the only individuals without an alibi were Grady, Steve, and Susie Andrews. It is obvious that these individuals have an internal alibi with each other.

From a psychological standpoint, this examiner found a lot of instability in Grady's and Susie's mannerisms and character. Based on an interview investigators had with Grady's ex-wife, Leigh Francis, she acknowledged that Grady was "obsessed with pornography." Janet stated that "both Grady and Susie would watch porno together, that Susie would walk in on Grady while he was masturbating and he would continue."

Leigh Francis acknowledged in her interview with investigators that Grady molested his brothers, Kevin and Frank Andrews. Francis claimed that Grady was "just sadistic" and "very malicious."

In the opinion of this examiner, Grady Andrews displaces his anger for Susie Andrews on everyone else but his mother, with whom he has developed a traumatic bond. That is, their attachment to each other is based upon the trauma one inflicts and the other accepts. The strength of this traumatic bond is demonstrated by the fact that 16 years after the murders, Grady Andrews still lives with his mother. In the opinion of this examiner, Grady would have done anything for his mother.

SIGNATURE BEHAVIORS

There very likely are two signature behaviors in these murders. The first signature action is the overall placement/pattern of the six gunshots. Each victim had one shot to the top of their heads. One victim had two shots to the side of his ear, and the other victim had two shots to the back of his head. In the opinion of this examiner, this pattern is the signature and may indicate a familiarity with guns. It may also suggest that the killer is a hunter. The second signature behavior, as previously mentioned, is the blunt force to Kevin's head, which indicates overkill.

RECOMMENDATIONS

In the opinion of this examiner, investigators should thoroughly investigate Susie and Grady Andrews for these murders before considering any other suspect. In the opinion of this examiner, a search of Susie Andrews's current residence would likely yield documents written by Grady Andrews similar to those discussed earlier in this report. This opinion is based on the examiner's analysis a poem that was written by Grady Andrews.

THE CASE PROFILE ANALYSIS WAS WRITTEN AND COMPLETED BY:

Dr. Maurice Godwin
Criminal Investigative Psychologist
Godwin Investigative Consultancy

I believe the solution to the case hinges on the poem written by eighteen-year-old Grady Andrews before his brothers' funeral:

A flower is a mirth,
And so taunt me on.
You flourished love,
On a vine,
Now you're gone.
Like the stars in the night,
Yet they appear again,
Have an enriched life,
Regretting no sin.

Using a computer linguistic program, I analyzed the poem's content. The linguistic program looks at the meanings of words in generic terms. Each line of the poem is entered into the computer and the meaning of the words and/or full statement is analyzed, with an explanation provided afterward. In this case, the poem was shown to be about infidelity.

The infidelity occurred between the mother, Susie Andrews, and her sons, Grady, Kevin, and Frank. Based on interview statements given by Susie Andrews, she had her favorite son, Grady, and often compared her sons' penis sizes. The devastation of Susie's incestuous acts helped contribute to the tension, anger, and jealousy between her sons. The sexual abuse coupled with Susie's having emotional control over her sons set the stage for the murders that occurred. I think Susie Andrews knew about the murders prior to their happening.

This poem reflects Grady Andrews's discombobulated state of mind, internal anger at Susie, and inexpressible rage. Grady's poem is unnaturally devoid of empathy for the situation or death of his brothers. Specifically, in the line, "A flower is a mirth," the word *flower* has no relevant meaning but rather is a diversion word. *Mirth* is the operative word.

Mirth is the psychological feature of experiencing euphoria. Grady had a feeling of euphoria all right, produced from terrible feelings of guilt; he disliked his brothers and the feeling was mutual. The affective aspect of Grady's actions was driven by rage and anger at his two brothers, Frank and Kevin.

Susie Andrews was the cause of the jealousy between the Andrews brothers and the subsequent murder of Frank and Kevin Andrews. Grady Andrews was losing control over Frank and Kevin; his ability to stop them from revealing their history of sexual molestation to others, such as the police, was coming to an end. I believe that Susie Andrews was having incest of one form or another with all of her sons, which eventually caused bitterness, jealously, anger, and rage among the brothers.

The line, "And so taunt me on," has a dual meaning. First, Grady is directing his anger at his mother. Susie often would punish and scold Grady. Grady had been controlled by his mother all of his life—both emotionally and sexually. This line in the poem also implies that Frank and Kevin were a threat to Grady and Susie.

So what, then, does "You flourished love on a vine," mean? At first glance, this line may appear to apply to Frank and Kevin. That, however, is not the case. Rather, the statement has implications that are directed at Susie. The mention of love implies Susie's love and the vine refers to her sons. "Now you're gone" means that two of the loves from the "vine" are now gone. Grady now feels a little safe and relieved from being revealed as a sexual deviant; so does Susie. It's their secret now.

"Like the stars in the night, yet they appear again." It's a beautiful line, isn't it? Here, Grady is talking about Frank and Kevin but he does not mean that they literally appear to him. Rather, he thinks about them in passing. As for, "Have an enriched life," notice the word "enriched" is present perfect tense.

Present perfect tense describes an action that happened at an indefinite time in the past or that began in the past and continues in the present. Here, Grady is wishing Frank and Kevin a good life in death.

Grady has no remorse for his actions. Note the last line, "Regretting no sin."

My conclusion, which I told the Pliskin cops, was that the poem was a confession of Grady's guilt, which was directed to his mother, Susie Andrews, to demonstrate that she was in control. It's like Grady was saying, "I'm on your side, Mom." The poem was not a confession to Susie that he committed the murders but rather a way for Grady personally to justify his actions to himself while trying, unsuccessfully as it turns out, to appear to others to have empathy.

It is up to the police now in Pliskin, Idaho, to make the case. The important thing is that new attention is centering on a double homicide. Perhaps with my profile, or some forensic evidence, this case can be cleared and the killers brought to justice.

CHAPTER 13

THE BTK SERIAL KILLER
THE MiAMi SERIAL RAPiST

*How many do I have to kill before I get my name in the paper
or some national attention?*
—BTK Strangler, *February 10, 1978*

AFTER THIRTY YEARS HE'S finally gotten his wish. Since March
of 2004 BTK has been reported on by every major news agency in
the United States. He's the topic of comment and speculation in
countless forums across the Internet. If you Google "BTK killer,"
you get over 5,000 hits. On May 29 he received one of the greatest
honors any publicity-loving criminal can hope for: his very own
profile on *America's Most Wanted.*

This is the story of the evil, psychotic murderer who stalks his
unsuspecting victims and has an ongoing and cordial relationship
with the press. He sends haunting letters and poems to the police
and the media, which are then followed by dramatic newspaper
headlines and countless "breaking news" segments on TV.

From the start, the case was sensational, but strip the theatrics
aside. It was obvious that a monster was on the loose. The first
murder came on January 15, 1974, when Wichita, Kansas, police
were dispatched to a house in Eastern Wichita. Young Charlie

Ortero had come home from junior high school and found his father and mother dead in their bedroom. Neighbors made the 911 call.

Police discovered Charlie's father, Joseph, bound with a Venetian blind cord, lying facedown in the bedroom. The mother, Julie, was bound in a similar fashion lying on the bed. As the officers continued to search the house, they found Charlie's nine-year-old brother, Joseph Otero II dead in his bedroom, similarly bound, with a plastic bag tied over his head. Officers later found eleven-year-old Josephine Otero hanging from the ceiling in the basement. All of the victims had been strangled with cord used in the making of Venetian blinds. The killer had evidently brought the cord to the house with him.

The autopsies revealed that none of the victims had been sexually assaulted. The daughter, Josephine, was found wearing only a sweater and socks, and crime technicians found semen in the basement and other areas of the house, indicating that the murderer had masturbated during or after the killings.

A task force investigation was launched. For days after the crime, seventy-five police officers fanned out across town and questioned over a thousand people. As time passed, more and more investigators were taken off the case and assigned to other duties. But the investigation continued and at one time three different men had confessed to the Otero killings. Evidently, BTK couldn't stand the thought of someone else getting the credit for what he had done. Even though police discredited all three confessions, the killer decided to make sure that the police knew he was still around and was definitely not one of the men who had confessed.

BTK phoned the tip hotline set up by the *Wichita Eagle-Beacon,* as that newspaper was called at the time. BTK informed the paper that more information on the Otero case could be obtained by retrieving a letter that had been placed in an engineering textbook that could be found on the shelves at the Wichita Public Library. It was quickly retrieved.

The letter started out with the words *THE OTERO CASE* in block letters. Not only did the author of the letter claim credit for the killings, but he also included a rambling, supposed explanation of why the crimes were committed. It began:

> Those three dude you have in custody are just talking to get publicity for the Otero murders, They know nothing at all. I did it by myself and no ones help. There has been no talk either. . . . Lets put it straight.

This is the letter which gave the killer his name, BTK. At one point he writes:

> Since sex criminals do not change their M.O. or by nature cannot do so, I will not change mine. The code words for me will be . . . Bind them, Torture them, Kill them, BTK . . .

Only three months after the first murders, long before the killer began to communicate with police, BTK struck again. On April 5, 1974, Kathryn Bright and her brother Kevin arrived at her home and were confronted by a man with a gun. He had apparently entered the house by breaking out the window in the back door. The intruder forced Kevin to tie his sister to a chair then took him to another room.

When the killer tried to strangle Kevin by wrapping a cord around his neck, Kevin fought back. BTK shot him twice in the back, but Kevin managed to flee the house. When police arrived, however, the killer was gone. They found Kathryn, still tied to the chair, with three knife wounds in her abdomen. She died a short time later. Three years later, in March of 1977, BTK returned.

This time, he entered the home of Shirley Vian. Vian, according to her children, had not been feeling well, and on March 17 her two oldest children had stayed home from school. Sometime around noon, a man knocked on the door and forced himself into the house. Brandishing a gun, he locked the children in the bathroom. The children eventually freed themselves, only to find their mother dead, tied hand and foot on her bed with a plastic bag fastened over her head.

At first, there was some discussion as to whether the Vian murder had been committed by BTK. The children had been unharmed and two money orders had been stolen from the home. All doubt vanished, however, when the *Eagle-Beacon* was mailed a small index card with a poem that began: "SHIRLEY LOCKS, SHIRLEY LOCKS, WILT THOUGH BE MINE."

Later he explained about the children:

They were very lucky; a phone call save them. I was going to tape the boys and put platics bag over there head like I did Joseph, and Shirley. And then hang the girl. God-oh God what a beautiful sexual relief this would been . . .

The next murder was called in to dispatch by BTK himself. On December 9, 1977, a man called from a phone booth only six blocks away from the police station city hall. He told the 911 dispatcher: "Yes, you will find a homicide." He provided the address, and added, "Nancy Fox."

Fox was found in her home, dead, her body partially clothed. She had been strangled with a nylon stocking. Police did not connect the murder with BTK until local Channel 10 news received a letter from him.

After a thing like Fox, I come home and go about life like anyone else. And I will be like that until the urge hits me again. I'm sorry this happen to society; they are the ones who suffer the most. It's hard for me to control myself.

A year and a half went by and BTK was silent. The investigation bogged down. No suspects; no nothing. One night in the spring of 1979, sixty-three-year-old Fran Dreier arrived home at eleven in the evening to find that her home had been burglarized. She called the police, who treated the matter as a normal robbery until, that is, she received an envelope containing jewelry that had been stolen from her home, a sketch drawn by the intruder, and a poem. The poem told how disappointed he had been that she hadn't come home until late that night. He had planned to kill her.

Dreier got out of town fast, but not before informing police. As for BTK, he disappeared again, or so Wichita's citizens hoped. And then, after a long break, he reappeared. In March 2004, *The Wichita Eagle* newspaper received an envelope with the name Bill Thomas Killman in the return address. It contained a one-page letter along with the photocopy of a driver's license and photocopies of three pictures of a dead body.

The driver's license belonged to a woman named Vicki Wegerle. On September 16, 1986, Wegerle's husband came home from lunch and found her body. Her hands and feet had been bound and she had been strangled to death. The three photocopied photographs showed the victim's dead body, posed differently for each shot. Eighteen years after the fact, BTK was claiming his victim.

Police were back at square one, trying to catch a serial killer whose trail had long since grown cold. They do have several possible descriptions of BTK, but unfortunately, none of them have resulted in an arrested or even the development of a viable suspect.

Neighbors of the Otero family described a stranger in the neighborhood the morning of the murders as a white male with dark shaggy hair. The Oteros' car had been taken after the murders were committed and one neighbor reported seeing the car driven by a dark-complexioned male in a rumpled hat.

Kevin Bright described his assailant as a white male, about twenty-five years old.

The Vian children told police that the killer was a chubby, dark-haired man, around forty years old. And finally, a fireman who used the same pay phone right after BTK called police to report the Fox murder described him as about six feet tall with blondish hair.

Obviously, the descriptions don't give police much to go on. However, considering that the murders are at least thirty years old, one could assume that the serial killer was in his mid-twenties when he started killing and probably would be at least in his fifties today. Police have the tape of BTK's 1977 911 phone call, which was computer enhanced by a New York professor in 1979. It has been played numerous times through the years on radio and TV; it can be downloaded from the Internet from several different Web sites dedicated to the BTK killings.

All the murders except for the Wegerle murder took place in East Wichita. Of the five crimes, three took place during the day. Police believe the killer entered the Otero residence sometime around 9 A.M. The Bright family was attacked around 2 P.M. BTK entered the Vian home around noon. BTK chose not to wait until 11 P.M. for Fran Dreier, sparing the life of that intended victim.

Perhaps the most important clues are in the letters BTK sent to the police and media. Do the letters contain the link to the identity of BTK? I believe that it is the geography of the BTK crimes that tells us something about his mental maps, the way in which he traveled throughout Wichita. BTK is intimately familiar with the landscape near and around where his first several murders occurred.

I developed a geographical profile of the BTK in March 2004. Subsequently, I was interviewed by several TV stations in the Wichita area. The map below shows the anchor point identified by Predator as BTK's place of residence, former place of residence, place of employment, or the residence of a present or former girlfriend.

After you finish this book remember where you put it on the shelf. Check it occasionally and keep up with breaking developments in the BTK murders—you may already know where BTK is located, or at least used to be located.

Maybe the police in Wichita will soon find out too.

GEOGRAPHICAL PROFILE OF BTK SERIAL KILLER

Rectangle indicates 1 mile police search area
✗ indicates Killer's anchor point, 200–299 South Belmont St.

* * *

Not all of my consulting work involves serial murder. Sometimes it involves serial rape. From time to time, I have volunteered my services on a case that I felt needed to be solved, and fast. The Shenandoah serial rapist was one such case.

For a year, beginning with his first crime on September 17, 2002, a serial rapist terrorized the Shenandoah and Little Havana neighborhoods of Miami. Detectives were slow to link the rapes to the same man, but once they did, no one in Little Havana or Shenandoah felt safe.

The rapist went after women ranging in age eleven to seventy-nine. He struck on random days during the day and at night. He raped seven women and attempted to rape three more. He spoke only in Spanish to his victims. Based on his accent, authorities suspected he was either Honduran or Nicaraguan.

In June 2003, Clear Channel Outdoor, a billboard company, donated more than two hundred posters and billboards with sketches of the rapist based upon victims' accounts. Police took more than two hundred DNA samples from men who matched the serial rapist's physical description. The city had received hundreds of tips on the rapist. A task force was formed to hunt the predator down. Nothing seemed to work; the police were stymied.

Reynaldo Elias Rapalo, thirty-two, was feeling pretty good.

The five-foot-two-inch Rapalo had been a construction worker. A native of Honduras, he was living in Miami on an expired visa at the time of the rapes. Just one month after the first rape, Miami police actually arrested Rapalo on charges of lewd and lascivious molestation on a child under twelve. A month later, prosecutors inexplicably dropped the charges.

Making up for lost time, Rapalo got himself arrested in July 2002 on an aggravated assault charge. His landlord, Cecilia Jimenez, bailed him out of jail. Eventually, she asked him to leave, because he kept coming home late, each time with different women on his arm. Rapalo, a regular churchgoer, became violent when Jimenez asked him to leave. After several threats, Rapalo made one real when he smashed the window of her Toyota 4-Runner. Jimenez called police.

When I became involved in the Shenandoah serial rapist case in August 2003, I saw the difficulty the police were having in making an arrest. I knew a geographical profile would help. An objective, scientifically designed geographic profile of the killer was in order, so, using the rape locations, I developed one. This time around, I didn't develop a criminal profile. I had great confidence that Predator would zero in on the guy.

Several days after developing my geographical profile, I contacted the Miami Police Department to offer the results to the investigators. My offer to help fell flat; I never heard back from the Miami Police Department, but I still felt the need to get my geographical profile out in order to save future victims from sexual assaults.

In early September 2003, a story on the unsolved rapes, featuring my profile, was published in the Spanish edition of the *Miami Herald*. If the task force investigating the rapist who stalked Miami's southeast neighborhoods raping children and women had relied on my geographical profile, chances are Reynaldo Elias Rapalo would have been detected and arrested earlier than he was. Instead the case was solved the way serial rapes and murders usually are—by luck.

Sergeant Will Golding of the Miami Police Department was doing surveillance on another rape case when he saw something that just wasn't right. There was a man driving slowly through the Little

Havana neighborhood in a faded 1993 black Mazda. Two blown stop signs later, Sgt. Golding pulled the driver over at Southwest 13th Avenue and 11th Street in Shenandoah.

When the man stopped his car, he flipped on the blinking hazard lights—something the serial rapist had done in a previous attack, Golding recalled. Realizing that he might have pulled over the serial rapist, he carefully checked the man's driver's license. His name was Reynaldo Elias Rapalo.

Rapalo had had numerous addresses, including one in the heart of Little Havana. Ostensibly arrested for the traffic violation, Rapalo voluntarily submitted to a DNA test that matched evidence recovered from the rapes. He has since been charged in the rapes and his case is pending trial as of this writing.

MIAMI RAPIST GEOGRAPHICAL PROFILE

Shaded wedge indicates recommended search area
Anchor hit area 0.9 miles from Rapalo Apt.

The geographical profiling map submitted to the Miami Police Department predicted an anchor hit area just nine-tenths of a mile from Rapalo's apartment at 1538 SW Sixth Street. The area where Golding pulled Rapalo over was near his former Sixth Street address. Rapalo had just recently moved from the Sixth Sreet location to southwest Miami-Dade, in a neighborhood west of Miami Metrozoo. The use of my profile early on would have pinpointed his home base area before he moved.

Rapalo's Sixth Street address is in the wedge, which is represented by the shaded area on the map. Considering the size of Miami, this profile is very accurate and supports my wedge theory; that is, that the offender's home will likely fall within a wedge-shaped area determined by the locations of the crime scenes. This narrows the potential search area for police.

The predicted anchor hit location is an exact address, which is rare in geographical profiling; more often, a general area is proposed. The anchor hit area shown on the map is representative of the hit area derived from probability percentages calculated achieved by my Predator system. In the end, of course, it does no good to create a geographical profile, no matter how accurate it is, unless law enforcement uses it.

EPILOGUE

THE DRU SJODIN CASE

WHEN A CASE IS finally solved, and the killer has been named and charged, there is usually partial closure for the victim's family. While the trial has not yet occurred, the system is bringing the (alleged) killer to justice. But what happens when you don't have a body to provide that ultimate closure? The most profound pain imaginable is that of a parent who has lost a daughter or son but has no body to complete the mourning.

This is often the result in cases where children are abducted. Unless the case is solved and the child located in the first seventy-two hours, the odds are that if the child is located at all he or she will be dead. Of course, just because a child is abducted doesn't make it a serial killer case. No matter what you see in the movies, the majority of child abductions are not done by serial criminals. This misperception is usually the result of local media reporting in the most sensational manner on the most sensational stories happening locally and regionally.

The national media gave Dru Sjodin little or no copy. It was the regional press in the Great Plains states that picked up on the story and wouldn't let it die until Dru Sjodin's body was recovered. But the real story in the Dru Sjodin case of 2004 really starts many years ago in a small northwestern Minnesota town, Crookston, home to Alfonso Rodriguez Jr.

Some of Rodriguez's friends would have profound memories of growing up with him. Some would remember him as the kind of kid who was the cautious one in a group of hell-raisers. That caution seemed to change when he became an adult.

Born in Laredo, Texas, Rodriguez moved to Crookston with his family in 1963. His father, Alfonso Sr., and mother, Dolores, were hardworking people who planted roots in the community. They performed manual labor in the fields, picking produce for money. Dolores cared for her young children, cooked, cleaned, and washed all the family's clothes by hand. The family joined a local Catholic church. Alfonso Sr. was illiterate in English. He managed to amass enough capital that he could invest it in a radiator repair shop. Dolores would eventually get a job cooking at cafés, which led to a kitchen job and more steady work at the University of Minnesota's local campus. The kids went to Crookston High School.

Ileana, the youngest, edited the school newspaper and was a cheerleader for the varsity basketball team. Daughter Rosa earned a master's degree. Sylvia, the oldest, moved to New York and worked for a doctor. Alfonso Jr., however, struggled. He struggled with schoolwork and he struggled with English, not becoming fluent until he was in his mid-twenties.

In school, Rodriguez was not a disciplinary problem. From all indications, his home life was no different than that of most American families. Rodriguez would recall for a psychologist in a 1976 psychological review that his memory differed from the popular perception of his home life. He said that he "tends to describe his home life as unpleasant, with parents who were critical of him and unreasonable in their demands."

As a teenager, Rodriguez dabbled in recreational drugs but nothing too heavy. He would cut class and hang out at the river, sometimes alone, sometimes with friends. He was the type who could be part of a group while not really being there, conservative, known as the "straight guy" of the group. Some of his friends found him quite boring.

Before his junior year in 1971, Rodriguez dropped out of high school. Two years later, he told therapists about depression headaches and acute anxiety. He said that he thought about sex when he was depressed or drinking. Rodriguez had hit his limit of feeling bad; it was time someone else did. Rodriguez began to channel his aggression into assaulting women.

First arrested in 1974, he pled guilty to separate counts of attempted rape and aggravated rape. Rodriguez told authorities that he had been seeking psychological help for the past three years. He knew it was only a matter of time before he got into "serious difficulties," he told a psychologist.

Sentenced to prison for up to fifteen years for that first assault, Rodriguez enrolled in a sex offender treatment program at the Minnesota Security Hospital in St. Peter. By 1978, he was released from the hospital and living in Mankato, Minnesota. His maximum sentence of fifteen years had turned into four years and out. Rodriguez lost no time in getting into trouble.

Arrested for rape, he was acquitted in 1979, whereupon he went home to Crookston. Crookston was none too happy to see his return. Wherever Rodriguez went trouble seemed to follow, and home was no exception. Rodriguez attacked a woman walking her dog in his neighborhood and tried to kidnap her. She was able to get away.

Rodriguez was convicted in 1980 of attempted kidnapping and first-degree assault for attacking a woman walking in her neighborhood. Rodriguez tried to explain his actions to the court: "Well, I had a problem of facing reality, facing growing up, feeling I didn't have too much of a good outlook on myself," he said. "I had a bad idea of my sexual identity at the time. And then I had a drinking problem besides, school problems. I didn't get along in school at all."

*　*　*

The judge asked him if he felt hostility toward women, Rodriguez replied, "In the past I did." This time, he went to prison for twenty-three years. When he was released from state prison in May 2003, he moved in with his mother in Crookston. Sometime toward the end of the year, authorities claim, he made the acquaintance of Dru Sjodin.

Dru Sjodin was a twenty-two-year-old college student attending the University of North Dakota in Grand Forks. Sjodin had just finished her shift at a lingerie store in a Grand Forks mall on November 22, 2003. She went out to the parking lot where she had parked her car. Talking on her cell phone to her boyfriend as she took out the keys to get in, the boyfriend heard her say "Oh my God" before the line went dead.

Dru went missing. On December 2, 2003, police charged Rodriguez with kidnapping her. By then, all hope of getting Dru back alive was practically gone, and Rodriguez wasn't talking. Without the body, prosecuting Rodriguez for her murder was far from a lock. Besides offering forensic evidence, the most important thing was to bring Dru back to her family. She had been missing for a couple of months when I was called in.

The Sjodin family had managed to recruit professionals to aid them in searching for Dru. They were all convinced that Rodriguez was the killer. He was just holding out and not telling anyone where she was. I was convinced that after the winter snows melted, we'd find her. That was what was slowing up locating her; the weather.

The chief of the approved search team contacted me. He had an unusual request: could I create a reverse geographic profile? A reverse geographic profile is using the crime locations such as abduction site, offender's home address, and work address, and, in Sjodin's case, a shoe found under a bridge, to predict where her body is. The idea was to pinpoint the location of the body and the general search area.

SJODIN REVERSE GEOGRAPHICAL PROFILE

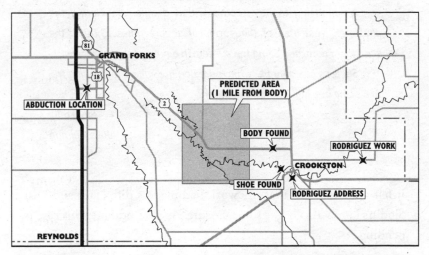

Armed with the map, search teams fanned out after the snows melted in April 2004. This was the first time that I know of that a geographical profile was used to predict where a body could be found. Dru was finally found west of Crookston, Minnesota, on Saturday, April 17. The predicted area was one mile from where the body was located, not bad at all considering how large a geographical area was being profiled.

One of the search team leaders subsequently sent me this letter:

Dr. Godwin:

Again, thank you for your contribution to the effort. You are a refreshing symbol of kindness and caring, standing far above your peers by your generosity.

It takes a hell of a man to risk your professional reputation by attempting to apply a science in a manner which has never been tried before. Hopefully, you will be able to refine it even more and this will become a standard tool in similar cases in the future.

It's amazing to have come within a mile considering the absolutely vast area of thousands of square miles (3,000), the scarcity of data, and using the system in a previously untried way!

Success can only be achieved if you are willing to actually try, and some are 'mo' willing than others.

Sincerely,

Jake Holman

It felt good to know that my work had made a difference and Dru Sjodin's family finally got some closure. As for Rodriguez, his case is pending.